From
BARISTA
to
BOARDROOM

From

BARISTA

to

BOARDROOM

*Lessons about Life and Leadership
from a Career in Coffee*

A MEMOIR

CHRISTINE C. McHUGH

CMC

Published by CMC, Seattle
www.christinemchughconsulting.com

Edited and designed by Girl Friday Productions
www.girlfridayproductions.com

Cover design: Rachel Marek
Project management: Katherine Richards and Laura Dailey
Image credits: cover © Mikhail Turov/Shutterstock, © Maryana
Kankulova/Shutterstock, © Natee Jitthammachai/Shutterstock

ISBN (hardcover): 978-1-7365581-1-9
ISBN (paperback): 978-1-7365581-0-2
ISBN (ebook): 978-1-7365581-2-6

Library of Congress Control Number: 2021904543

First edition

For Tate and Nick, the loves of my life

PROLOGUE

As I stood outside the Starbucks Support Center, looking up at the clock tower, I saw the green-and-white siren perched atop, smiling at me. It hit me—I would never again enter the doors as a Starbucks "partner." I shook with sadness, and my stomach was in knots over how my last few hours of employment had unfurled. There hadn't been time to process it all yet, but I was ready for whatever came next.

My departure was quiet. I slipped out of the building unnoticed and loaded the last box into the trunk of my car. In just half an hour, I'd be having a celebratory glass of champagne with my husband, Tate, at a restaurant in Seattle's Pike Place Market.

I was incredibly proud of my twenty-seven-year career at Starbucks, where I started as a barista and rose to the level of vice president. I had spent over half my life there.

Pulling out of the garage, I peeked over my shoulder and took one last look at the siren, nodding a silent thank-you as I drove away.

It was the end of one era but the start of a new one. I was now officially a customer on the other side of the counter.

CHAPTER 1

We can let someone else write our story, or we can grab the pen and craft it ourselves. In my last few weeks at Starbucks, a friend at work reminded me that the narrative framing my resignation was mine to own. If I wasn't proactive and intentional about the messages surrounding my departure, others would fill in the details.

No matter how angry and resentful I was, I needed to take control—I was damned if I was going to let someone else write my script.

The end of my tenure was difficult. I felt bitter, undervalued, and underappreciated. I worked hard to keep it together those last days so I could leave with an air of dignity and self-respect to retain full ownership of my story.

Not long before I gave my notice, I met with my new boss, Andrew, about my role with the company. I was fresh off a company-sponsored sabbatical, and my department had been completely ripped apart while I was on leave.

The new job he laid out for me stank. It was as if it had been crafted out of thin air—ethereal strands of nothingness.

His effusive energy and optimism did little to minimize my disappointment in the lack of substance to the role. I sat there listening to him, searching for a scrap of meaningful work while his voice faded in and out. As I drifted, he began to sound like Charlie Brown's teacher talking to me. All I heard was "Wah wah wah."

It took everything within me to remain composed. I tried to distract myself from the crappy news by taking in the scrawl on the massive whiteboard that wrapped his office walls. It reminded me a bit of scenes from the movie *A Beautiful Mind* with its mess of random numbers and words that I'm sure meant something but, in that moment, looked like gibberish to me. After all, I'd been gone six months, and I had a lot of catching up to do.

It wasn't the department reorganization I was upset about—I was a seasoned executive and had plenty of experience leading complex structural changes. I often joked that reorganizing was one of Starbucks's areas of expertise. Change was in our ethos, and this meant partners (Starbucks's term for "employees") needed to be highly adaptive to new bosses and new work. It was exciting but also tiring because of the constant shifts and the need to ramp up in all dimensions with each change.

However, if you worked there for more than a few years, you grew accustomed to the constant shifts that came in a fast-growing company. People who didn't acclimate either left because it drove them crazy, or they were asked to leave because they couldn't keep up.

Right before I left for my sabbatical, I was the vice president of Customer Service and Operations Services. While I was gone, my position had been eliminated (the second time this happened to me while on an approved company leave), and my team had been dismantled and would now be the responsibility of executive teams from multiple departments. The customer contact center had been moved to another vice president as part of a new global strategy for the company.

The customer service programs and measurement part of my group were moved to another executive in Operations. And the operations consultation and planning teams went to yet another one of my peers in Operations.

I had anticipated things would change while I was out, but I never expected that there would no longer be a head of Customer Service at Starbucks. The idea was to signal that everyone in the company had a responsibility to be customer oriented.

I was highly skeptical that this would happen, though. My experience at Starbucks told me that without having a concentrated focus by a relentless leader, the impact of any effort would be lackluster and without staying power. I'd seen it happen previously with Diversity and Inclusion, Partner Experience, and Brand. A dedicated leader is needed to declare a position and company strategy and bring a strong voice to the table; otherwise, the message gets diluted and fractured.

I believe that when everyone's in charge, no one is.

I loved being responsible for Customer Service so much because customers are the reason businesses like Starbucks exist. Customers get attached to *their* store and *their* favorite barista. It's this personal connection that sets Starbucks apart from other restaurants and coffee shops.

Each week, partners in the stores served millions of customers and delivered millions of personal connections, and I was passionate about being an advocate for all of them. Every aspect of the customer experience fell under my scrutiny, from the way they were greeted at the register, to the accessibility of the bathrooms, to the ease of how the lids fit on the cups. If any of these things frustrated our customers or got in the way of baristas to serve them, I was like a terrier, hanging on until the issue shook free in resolution.

While some people might have shrunk away from disgruntled customers or become paralyzed when things went awry, I took great pride in taking care of the most frustrated customers, whose concerns made it to my desk by way of Starbucks's ceo, Howard Schultz. Often in a last-ditch effort, they would write or call him when no one else seemed able to solve their problem. Part of my job was to respond on his behalf.

My strength was that I genuinely cared enough to seek to understand where we fell short with their experience. My interactions were not motivated by protecting our brand reputation or preventing litigation, but out of fostering the personalized human connection that made Starbucks what it was. Ninety-nine percent of the time, the customer just wanted someone to listen, and I was good at that, even if it took an unexpected thirty minutes out of my day. I vividly remember the time a customer was extremely upset about how her experience with her service animal was handled by a barista who hadn't received training on situations like that. Through no fault of the barista, the customer left angry, the issue unresolved, resulting in an upset email that made it to my inbox. I called her and listened for twenty minutes. After I apologized and thanked her for bringing her concern to my attention, I shared what actions we were going to take. She was thankful and ended the call, indicating that she would go back to that store and continue to be a customer.

I carried my customer flag high, valiantly waving it to try to get everyone to care as much as I did. Internally, the customer experience was often described as how much money they spent each visit or how often they came in, missing an opportunity to talk about them as human beings. Care and compassion for humanity was one of the foundations Starbucks was built on.

I recorded phone calls to the call center so that others could listen to them. My hope was that hearing the emotion in the customer's voice would generate empathy and, ultimately, a desire to change a policy, practice, or product for the better. I asked departments and team leaders to read customer stories at the weekly coffee-tasting rituals to remind us why we were all there—to serve the customer.

With neighboring customer-obsessed companies like Amazon and Nordstrom in Seattle setting the standard for service, advocating for customers felt like an oddly uphill battle at Starbucks.

It seemed contrary to a company built on relationships, but the organization tended to be more product and partner centric than customer centric. Before I came into my customer service role, policies were put in place to address the minute percentage of people who misused our stores, taking advantage of our welcoming space for activities not connected to buying coffee and connecting with friends. Photos in company materials contained images of nothing but beautifully designed locations with no customers in them. Baristas were encouraged to become Coffee Masters and product experts, even if it meant doing a coffee tasting while excluding the customers sitting at the table next to them. These were all small things, but part of a paradigm shift I hoped to create by putting "Customer Service" in my job title.

Over the course of my tenure as vp of Customer Service, I helped drive a change in company culture. We revisited the restroom-usage policy and made them available to anyone whether an in-store purchase was made or not. Photos of customers and baristas interacting with one another were added to training materials and started getting added to presentations. A new module was added to the Coffee Master program to include a customer-connection component. These were not revolutionary actions but small steps forward to signal what was important.

But it all unraveled when I went on sabbatical.

Andrew became my boss while I was on leave. He and I knew each other from working on a few projects together in the past, most notably the Starbucks card and the Starbucks app. We had a good, collaborative relationship, and when I first learned about his new role, I looked forward to working with him.

Prior to joining Operations, he accomplished other noteworthy results in his technology role at Starbucks. His childlike enthusiasm, high energy, creativity, and likability created a lot of fans at the senior-executive levels and on Wall Street.

He had a quasi-"golden child" status at the time, virtually untouchable, in part due to his reputation for bringing innovative business-growth ideas into the company (mobile order-and-pay is one example). He effectively connected the baby boomers running the company to the needs and desires of the millennial and Gen Z customers who walked through our doors, which not many other Starbucks executives could do.

I knew going in he didn't exactly have a reputation for developing great teams or leaders, but this wasn't so unusual for Starbucks at the time. I saw plenty of smart, boundary-pushing executives lauded for their breakthrough thinking even if they weren't good people leaders.

Over the previous decade, Starbucks started to prioritize those characteristics over great leadership skills when it came to talent management and promotions. This frustrated me, given that during most of my career, Starbucks had high regard for relationship building and taking care of people, values I prided myself in. It was never said overtly, but I sensed that those things weren't so important to the company anymore. Perhaps the culture had evolved, and I hadn't quite caught up.

That day in Andrew's office, I grew dizzy looking at the whiteboard on his wall and tried to focus by pushing away the "wah wah" talk. I scrunched my forehead and searched hard for something concrete in the role he was offering me. But what he described felt just like the box sketched out on the org chart—empty. I tried to match his excitement for the future, but I just couldn't muster it without feeling completely dishonest with him and, more important, with myself.

"What exactly do you see my role doing, and how do you envision me contributing to the organization?" I asked skeptically, practicing patience (not one of my strengths).

Andrew replied confidently. "Helping bridge the gap between the international operations teams and the US operations team. The international teams don't feel like they're getting a good level of service."

"How come the US operations teams aren't able to do this, and why does everyone think a middleman is needed?" I remained doubtful and wondered if Andrew really thought this was the right solution.

"It's just not top of mind for the US team. I don't know exactly why it's not happening or what is needed. This is why I need you to figure it out," said Andrew enthusiastically.

I wasn't convinced. I'd been around long enough to know that any "go-between" role like he described would be extremely frustrating and eventually become a risk for position elimination. No one wants to work within a bureaucratic framework like that, and eventually people realize it makes more sense to just work directly with one another like they should have in the first place. In my opinion, it was a total waste of company resources and simply didn't have staying power.

No matter how hard Andrew tried to spin the role as the possibility to create something new, I just couldn't get excited about it. I pictured myself withering away in a dark corner of the building, feverishly working to make something out of nothing in order to justify my existence. It went against my ethics—I like to have purpose and meaning and to be productive, not just to bide my time.

Was this my payback for going on sabbatical? I'd had this awesome, personally enriching time off, and I came back to a shit sandwich.

Sure, a sabbatical might sound like a great perk, but it often came with mixed messages, especially for executives. Asking for one could be construed as lacking loyalty or commitment. Sometimes executive sabbaticals were the company's idea, used to cover for a performance-management issue and a way to prepare for a future transition out. I knew that it was a risk when I requested the time off, but part of me thought I might be able to defy the odds.

About two months before I was scheduled to return, I had a phone conversation with my boss, Sara, in which she told me that Andrew would be my new boss when I got back. I loved working with her and knew I was going to miss her a lot because she was a great manager for me.

While relatively young for her position, she had an incredible knack for navigating the politics and personalities required for successful executives at Starbucks. She demonstrated great patience and just the right amount of impatience at the same time. Her energy, positivity, candor, and empathy always made you feel cared for but also made it clear what was expected. Her expectations were high, but that made you want to work harder and smarter in order to meet them.

Sara's petite frame was usually adorned in clothes that looked like they were purchased at a local boutique. A favorite ensemble was a stylish, loose-fitting top with clean lines paired with chic pants and accessorized with tasteful yet artistic jewelry. Her unruly dark curly hair had an attention-getting white streak in the front that people always asked if she colored because it was so dramatic. (The answer was no.) She was comfortable with who she was but didn't stray so far to the edge that people at all levels in the organization couldn't relate to her.

We had known each other for at least ten years, having collaborated on various projects together. When she first relocated to Seattle, before she was my boss, we would go running at lunch, and it was a great way to catch up about our kids and work, giving us both a needed break in the day. Our relationship was not intimate or social outside of the office, but we felt an ease and comfort around one another.

As we caught up on the phone, she gave me a hint of what things were going to be like when I returned from my sabbatical. Not only was Andrew now my boss, but my position had been eliminated. I was disappointed for sure because I loved the customer service work, but all I wished for was a meaningful role aligned with my strengths.

"So, Christine, have you given any more thought to what you want to do when you get back? We didn't want to slot you into anything specific as we'd figured you could ease back in and be involved in determining where you land," she explained.

I knew with the highest level of clarity what I wanted to do. But would Starbucks have that available for me? Prior to going on sabbatical, I had spent about six months working with a career coach—paid for by Starbucks—to help me solidify and articulate the type of work where I excelled.

The process was both empowering and liberating, but, when all was said and done, I couldn't find a job internally that matched my strengths. When I learned that the customer service piece that I loved so much was taken away while I was on sabbatical, I started to get discouraged. Would I ever find a place that felt right?

My answer to Sara's question had a clarity I hadn't been able to articulate in decades: I wanted to leverage my strengths of serving others, driving and owning major cross-functional work, leading a team in a nontechnical function, and directly impacting partners and customers.

Sara responded in her typically direct manner. "You know, Christine, that probably won't exist when you get back, so you're going to have to agitate people. You'll need to remind them what you're good at and stay in front of them."

I felt my face get hot and my hands start to shake at her word "agitate." I appreciated her honesty, but I became agitated just *hearing* the word.

I was incredulous. I had worked at Starbucks for twenty-seven years, yet people didn't know what I was good at, so I'd have to remind them? Really? It wasn't like I was a poor performer who had skated by all these years—I had more than demonstrated my willingness and ability to move around, based on where the company needed me.

At that moment, I started to wonder if the writing was on the wall, but no one wanted to tell me directly. Passive-aggressive behavior was an unspoken but well-known cultural blemish Starbucks bore.

I was coming back to a nonexistent role, given the recent reorg, and I was going to have to stir things up just to get people to pay attention to me. Why make me go through these gyrations? Why not just give me a severance package?

When people leave Starbucks, it's cynically called being "promoted to customer." I started to speculate that might be what was next for me. After all, my job was eliminated; there was no known role for me at the time; and I would be costing the company money biding my time, waiting for the right job.

I hung up the phone, hurt and angry, but I knew I had to go back, even if just temporarily. I needed a job and an income to support my family, and it was going to have to be at Starbucks—at least for the time being. I had just taken six months off unpaid, and I couldn't go without a paycheck much longer.

When I got back, the meeting with Andrew told me what I needed to know. While Sara had led me to believe that I'd have time to figure out what might be next for me and that the organization would be supportive, Andrew sketched out a vague role that was made to sound important. But there was nothing substantial to it.

I put on my game face and thanked him for holding a spot on the org chart for me. But I also shared with him that the ethereal job he offered me was missing the critical elements that were important to me.

I know he could see and feel my lack of enthusiasm, but he didn't seem to have much energy for helping me figure out other options. He was obviously distracted by the demands of the business, settling the recent reorg, and learning his own new role.

I had a feeling that I was merely another thing to concern himself with, and he didn't have the mindshare or, frankly, in my opinion, the genuine interest to help me move forward. I listened to him talking excitedly about the work of my peers, but I felt a noticeable lull in his energy when it came to what he envisioned for me.

I was nervous that I might be falling into a category of former long-term partners who became perceived as entitled or not open to change. I had seen some of these people stagnate as the company evolved around them, and then, suddenly, their talents or their work became irrelevant.

If I couldn't make sense of Andrew's ask and create a job and work plan for myself out of thin air, was I now one of *them*? I never took a single moment at Starbucks for granted and worked hard every day to prove myself—resting on my laurels was not part of my DNA. But did my colleagues or leadership see me this way? A panic was starting to set in, and signs that this was no longer a place for me became increasingly abundant.

While Andrew tried to figure out what to do with me, I tried to figure out what to do, period.

I explored other parts of the organization to see if there might be roles down the road that were a good fit for me. A few executives reached out to me about potential opportunities, but none of them lit me up. I wanted my body to vibrate with an overwhelming desire to go for it—but I just didn't feel it. My restlessness was growing, and I'd only been back a week.

I channeled some of my time and energy doing what I loved most—opening my door to career- and leadership-coaching conversations with whoever needed them.

Partners came to me for advice on how to work better with their boss or how to navigate through organizational politics, given all the recent change. Some came to me for career advice because they couldn't see their future, or they were feeling underutilized.

My advice was always the same: "Live your values and speak your truth. That's all that matters."

It was advice I needed to heed myself.

I tried to keep busy by attending Andrew's team meetings, edging my way into conversations, offering my opinions on the strategies and tactics at play, grasping for a purpose, and trying desperately to add *something*.

Before I went on leave, I was one of Sara's trusted advisers. Now, someone else had stepped into that role with Andrew, and I watched the rest of my peers jockeying for position.

I could swear that my ideas fell on deaf ears. It felt like everyone was harboring a secret, and I was the only one who didn't know what it was. I had been gone only six months, but it felt like my sabbatical wiped out the previous twenty-seven years of Starbucks experience. I was clearly in the outer circle now, and I was frustrated trying to find my way back in.

In the "wah wah" meeting, Andrew asked me to come back to him with my thoughts on a job description and what I proposed the business needed. Our conversation was pleasant enough but cut short because he needed to take a phone call—another sign that I was not a priority, and I was dismissed as what felt like a busy-work assignment.

As I closed his door behind me, my hands shook, and my stomach started roiling.

I kept my eyes down as I walked briskly to my office across the building. I was so afraid that I would burst out crying if I saw anyone I knew. I'd been back only two weeks, but I wasn't sure how much longer I could endure the boredom, the not feeling valued, and not being a part of anything.

Once I reached my office, I closed the door, lowered the blinds, and let the tears flow. I didn't want anyone to see what a mess I was. I mean, shouldn't I have been happy that I just had six months off to do whatever I wanted? Sabbaticals were designed to recharge and renew, but coming back to Starbucks without a set job felt depleting.

I took a few deep breaths to try to calm down, but I desperately needed to talk to someone—a trusted confidant who could help me process what I was feeling. My emotions and energy were so raw, and I was worried that, if I didn't find a way to blow off steam, I would lose my composure.

But I had to be careful about whom I talked with—unloading with the wrong person could potentially backfire on me. There were always optics to consider at the executive level.

I decided to text my good friend Michelle, another senior executive in the company whose office was two floors below mine. She knew me well, and I trusted her.

Michelle and I had met when I was in the Starbucks Sales division. We had known each other for over twenty years and met at work, but our friendship deepened when we became next-door neighbors after she moved to Seattle from Chicago. We literally shared a hedge that served as a fence between our houses, and we would often have impromptu Sunday family dinners, each bringing whatever we had in the fridge.

Michelle and her husband are both hardworking and accomplished professionals but take everything in stride. Despite their busy lives, they never seemed frenetic or stressed, which always had me in awe. On occasion, their nanny would take our son, Nick, with them on excursions, giving him time with Michelle's two kids who became the siblings he never had.

As our kids got older, we started to take family trips together. There was an ever-present natural ease that made traveling fun. Our friendship grew as our lives became enmeshed in day-to-day living and adventure-filled vacations. Eventually, we asked Michelle and her husband to be guardians for Nick if anything happened to us.

Outside of our friendship, I held Michelle in high professional regard for being a great leader.

As the head of Starbucks Food Service and Licensing Sales division, she was well respected for her great business sense and people-leadership skills and had a real knack for navigating organizational politics without getting stymied by them.

I actually think she liked the thrill of being able to attack tough problems and sway difficult personalities. I'm confident she genuinely loved the art of the negotiation, whether it be with external customers or with colleagues in the office. She dressed the part of sophisticated salesperson when the time called for it, but her quasi-bohemian style and wry smile would win everyone over to lock it all in.

Luckily, when I texted Michelle right after I left Andrew's office, she was available. I practically ran down the two flights of stairs to her office, avoiding eye contact with everyone I passed on the way. When I rounded the corner to her office, her assistant nodded me in without a word.

I shut the door, and the waterworks started again.

Michelle thoughtfully had me turn my back to her window so people walking by couldn't see my face and how upset I was. Not only was she thinking about my privacy, but she knew that a crying executive could spark speculation, or even worse, convey weakness. Leaders are supposed to be strong and be able to hold it together.

I immediately unloaded on her while she listened attentively and with compassion.

"I'm so frustrated, I just want to quit now! I'm so fucking done with this place!"

Michelle offered me a Kleenex. "Listen, I know this is rough," she said calmly, looking me in the eye, "but you are likely going to be leaving here at some point, so use this time to go out with your head held high. Take control of your story, and don't let anyone else write it for you."

I paused. I felt caught between a rock and a hard place. We both knew that a rash decision wouldn't serve me or my family well, but she was right—blowing up now was the wrong move.

Michelle's comment put the power back in my hands. No matter how miserable I was, I didn't have to let this experience own me and define me. It was my story and destiny, not anyone else's.

I thanked her with a hug. Then, I wiped the tears from my face and checked my makeup in her mirror to make sure I looked somewhat presentable.

Leaving her office, I walked taller, with my chin up and my dignity replenished.

Serendipitously, the next day I was offered a job at a health and wellness start-up as the chief strategy officer. The job had all the things I was looking for in my next move, including a lot of autonomy. The pay and benefits weren't as robust as Starbucks's, but the biggest deciding factor was having the opportunity to work with like-minded people where I felt valued and appreciated. To be able to make a difference.

It felt like a huge leap but one that I was ready for. Because, if not now, then when?

I gave Andrew my two weeks' notice, and, when my resignation was announced, a crush of people stopped by my office to say goodbye. I felt a tinge of relief to be moving on and was excited about what was next, but there was also some sadness.

I had spent so many of my waking hours at Starbucks and had met my dearest friends there. My husband, Tate, and I had met via a Starbucks connection, and our son was in the on-site day care his first few years. The company had become a huge part of my identity and my life, and I was now putting that chapter behind me.

Energized about my future, I made the rounds to select senior leaders to share what I was doing next and to thank them. In the spirit of owning my story, I wanted them to hear firsthand from me why I was leaving. This lessened the risk of a convoluted message if they heard about it from a third party.

I was one of the most tenured people in the company, had been on some very high-profile projects, and had a strong reputation as a culture keeper. People constantly looked to me for advice on navigating the organization, and I was asked to mentor new executives coming in. My influence and imprint on the company were far wider and deeper than I could have ever imagined. Going out with my head held high was not just important to me, but also to those I was leaving behind.

As my last day rolled around, I had butterflies in my stomach again, this time a mix of nerves and excitement.

It was the day of our department's weekly coffee tasting where we talked about the business, key projects, and people updates. I figured there would be a couple of minutes for me to say thank you and goodbye to the team as the coffee tasting was the perfect forum for such announcements.

I gathered up my thoughts and listened to Andrew share some pertinent business announcements. He brought his usual high energy and almost levitated off the floor as he expressed confidence that his team was on the right track with the work that they were doing.

Then, as was customary, he turned it over to the group for any other announcements or recognition, at which point different team members shared important project milestones before welcoming a new partner to the team.

The updates wound down, and, as the group started to disperse, I thought for sure he or someone would say something to acknowledge my last day. I was standing right up front, and he looked directly at me.

Instead, it was crickets. No one said anything.

Maybe Andrew forgot; maybe he didn't know it was my last day; or maybe he didn't care, but the fact that he said nothing told me everything.

After twenty-seven years and more than half of my life, my time at Starbucks had come to an end.

I walked swiftly back to my office and did everything in my power to keep the tears at bay. With my hands shaking, I texted some friends in desperation and asked them to help me pack up the remaining items in my office and help me carry them out to my car.

As I scanned my partner badge to exit the garage for the last time, I glanced up at the siren with a flood of emotion.

I had been officially promoted to customer.

CHAPTER 2

Two days after I graduated from high school, I disembarked the plane at Sea-Tac International Airport, ready to start a new life in the big city of Seattle. It was four months before my eighteenth birthday, and one of my graduation presents was a one-way ticket out of my hometown of Fairbanks, Alaska. It was all I wanted. A new adventure and an uncertain future were calling me.

As soon as I touched down in Seattle, my first order of business was to find a job and enroll in community college. I stayed with my mom for a few months while I got my footing and saved some money to get my own place.

I was no stranger to work, having had my first job when I was just twelve years old. My grandparents owned a retail gift shop in Fairbanks where they sold Alaskan handicrafts and other imported gift items, and I worked there in the busy summer tourist season.

I loved the idea of earning my own money to spend or save as I saw fit.

I grew up poor, raised by my dad after my mom left when I was four years old. My dad did his best to provide for our basic needs, and I know it wasn't easy for him to be a single father to two young kids. At times, he could barely manage, and, at one point, we lived in a relative's basement for a year because we couldn't afford a place of our own. But my little brother, Jason, and I had food, clothing, and the love of a large extended family nearby.

There wasn't any extra money for the things I loved like *Archie* comic books and Snickers bars at the local convenience store, movie tickets, or trips to Dairy Queen for butterscotch Dilly Bars. Instead of complaining about it, I persistently asked my relatives for ways to earn a buck and took whatever job or task I was offered very seriously.

I genuinely liked to work and couldn't wait to get a job in Seattle.

Not knowing exactly how to find work in the big city, I decided to pursue a profession I was most familiar with—a receptionist in a hair salon. This was what I did my senior year of high school, and I enjoyed serving the clients and getting my hair done for free.

The *Seattle Times* didn't yield much, so I picked up the *Yellow Pages* and started calling salons to ask if they were hiring. The first couple of places said they didn't have any openings, but the third one I called said someone had just quit and asked if I could come in that day. I figured it was better than an interview, so I put on my white denim skirt, sleeveless blue turtleneck sweater, and my low-heeled white synthetic pumps and was at their University District location in less than an hour.

As soon as I walked in the door, they threw me behind the desk with no training to see if I could handle it. I didn't know the stylists, how the schedule worked, or even how to ring people up. It was exhilarating and nerve-racking at the same time.

But after a little trial and error over the next couple of hours, I got the hang of it, and they offered me the job on the spot. I had my first job in Seattle within a week of my plane touching down at Sea-Tac, and I couldn't wait to start.

Working at the hair salon thrust me into Seattle's urban culture. The University District was a busy neighborhood filled with coffee shops, hippie-clothing stores, and vegetarian restaurants. College students, retail employees, and university staff flooded the sidewalks, and finding a parking spot was nearly impossible.

I was fascinated by the casual coolness of my coworkers at the salon. Their alternatively styled all-black clothes definitely didn't come from J. C. Penney. They had more piercings than I had ever seen, and one of the guys even wore makeup. They did each other's hair frequently, experimenting with colors and modern haircuts that I didn't see in Fairbanks—the land of curly perms and blond highlights, dated fashion trends that the rest of the country had left far behind.

Working at the salon was fun and a good indoctrination to Seattle, but I needed to make more money to be able to afford my own apartment. I was shocked at how expensive Seattle was compared to Fairbanks.

I quit after a year and started working for my mom as a manager at an espresso cart she owned at the Seattle Art Museum. The job offered me more pay, and the schedule would work better when I started at community college in the fall.

The coffee business was a phenomenon that I noticed when I first moved to Seattle. Unlike in Fairbanks, there was a plethora of specialty coffeehouses and portable carts on pretty much every street corner.

One of Seattle's original coffee shops, Cafe Allegro (founded by Dave Olsen, retired Starbucks chief coffee buyer), was in the same building as the salon where I worked. I watched in fascination as my coworkers made the trek downstairs to get their daily fix.

They'd come back with big smiles on their faces, anticipating the decadent-looking drinks that smelled heavenly and were overflowing with fluffy whipped cream. Soon enough, I was hooked on caffè mochas and habitually popped in through Allegro's back door to grab a cup of coffee on my way into work.

It was the late eighties, and enterprising entrepreneurs capitalized on the growing coffee-by-the-cup industry with the start-up investment costs for street carts low, making it easy for virtually anyone to get in on the trend. A stop for a morning cup of joe was quickly becoming part of the daily routine for commuters.

The city chamber and visitor center had printed maps for self-guided coffee tours that included Starbucks, Monorail Espresso, and Espresso Vivace. Tourists now had more to see than the Space Needle and Pike Place Market—Seattle was getting on the map for its burgeoning coffeehouse culture.

My mom was one of the people who wanted to get in on this highly profitable business and purchased two espresso carts of her own, one of which was located at the Seattle Art Museum (where I worked) and the other in a medical office in Tacoma.

Working at the museum exposed me to a side of Seattle I hadn't yet experienced. From the distinguished-looking museum patrons to the quirky security guards who were my main customers, to the crush of Volunteer Park–goers who turned me into an Italian-soda-making machine when the sun came out, I was exposed to them all. It was urban neighborhood culture, and the city art scene mashed up into one big kaleidoscope of diversity.

I really enjoyed making espresso and serving customers, and it was while working at my mom's espresso cart that I first heard about Starbucks.

We used Starbucks espresso as our beans of choice, and, on occasion, our account rep, Jennifer, stopped by to see how things were going and if we needed anything.

I liked the taste of the coffee, and I'd heard from a few people that Starbucks was a good company to work for with generous benefits, although I'd never been inside any of their cafés. I thought they were only for cool hipsters or coffee geeks, neither of which category I fit into.

On the occasion that I walked by one of their stores on Capitol Hill where I lived, I peered inside to see the cozy environment decorated with natural woods. I could always hear jazz or classical music playing if the door was open.

I finally made enough money to move into an apartment with a roommate and decided to quit my mom's business to look for another job closer to school.

After class one day, I popped into the campus job-placement center and noticed a posting on the bulletin board for Starbucks baristas at a new store opening nearby. I had the right background, and the location was much more convenient than driving downtown to the museum, so I copied the information from the index card and called the hiring manager that day.

We agreed to meet at the Oak Tree Starbucks, a high-volume commuter store in a strip mall on a busy north-south thoroughfare in Seattle. It was across the parking lot from a movie theater and an upscale grocery store I patronized when I felt like I could afford a splurge. Their homemade croutons were one of my favorite purchases. I'd buy a container and eat them as if they were potato chips, often my only meal of the day.

The hiring manager started the interview with a French press of coffee, which I would come to learn was a tradition at Starbucks.

I followed her lead of smelling, then slurping the coffee and tried to put words to what I was tasting like she did. I couldn't pick out any distinguishing flavors and burned my tongue in the process, but fully participated as if I knew what I was doing.

My interview went well, and she offered me the job on the spot.

I officially became a Starbucks barista on July 13, 1989. I was just nineteen years old and, little did I know at the time, witnessing the beginning of something that would become very, very big.

I trained at a variety of stores over the summer while mine was being built. It was fun to be in different neighborhoods and to experience the diversity of customers. I spent some time at a downtown high-rise called the Columbia Center, which was, at the time, the tallest building on the West Coast.

It was crazy busy and fast-paced, filled with office workers dressed in professional attire I hoped to wear myself someday. I didn't see myself staying in retail forever.

Most of the business was for to go, and drip coffee, followed by handcrafted espresso drinks, was among the most popular. Today's hugely popular Frappuccino Blended Beverages did not exist yet, and the only cold drinks you could get were an iced latte, Americano, or mocha.

The store had two espresso bars designed to handle the long lines, and the sound of steaming milk and the nonstop espresso grinder was almost deafening. Baristas had to shout orders to one another as there weren't sticker printers yet or even check boxes printed on the cups to identify the customer's drink of choice. The baristas impressed me with their ability to keep it all straight in their heads, seeming to thrive on the cacophony and organized chaos.

The Columbia Center was a stark contrast to University Village (a.k.a. U Village, Seattleite shorthand for the upscale outdoor shopping center), another store I trained at that summer. Opened in 1972, U Village was Starbucks's second store, and the clientele knew a whole lot about coffee, often challenging my own knowledge.

They came in dressed in their Seattle plaid with their reusable coffee bags in hand, eyeing new baristas skeptically over fogged glasses, evidence of the rainy days Seattle is known for.

Even though there was no seating at the time, the U Village store invited intellectual conversation with the staff about coffee and politics in the warmth of its dark wood decor. The back counter was lined with jars of spices, loose leaf teas, bulk chocolate, chicory, and candied ginger, which we weighed on a scale before wrapping in brown paper.

When the occasional customer purchased a coffee beverage along with their beans, it was usually an Americano or a doppio espresso, revealing their coffee-purist proclivities. Mochas were popular only on Mondays because they cost only a dollar, which justified the splurge for something more indulgent.

By the time my store opened in North Seattle, I had completed two months of training and was eager to root myself in one place.

Even though our store was a small kiosk inside a grocery store, we had just as much pride as the baristas at Columbia Center and University Village. Opening a brand-new store was exciting in and of itself, but we were also part of an experimental concept. The smaller format was born out of a partnership with a local grocer that allowed Starbucks to increase the number of stores without the real estate and construction costs.

I'd arrive at 5:00 a.m. to prep the store for our first customers who usually showed up just before 5:30 a.m. My alarm abruptly went off at 4:15. I shrugged into my work uniform of white shirt and black pants and made my way to my car, still half-asleep.

Except in the summer, the twenty-minute drive to the store was pitch-black at that hour. I rubbed my bleary eyes to stay focused on the road and made myself an Americano once I arrived.

I loved being a barista, and I reveled in working the early-morning opening shift. Once the caffeine started coursing through my veins, I looked forward to being that bright spot in the beginning of each customer's day.

Just as the air began to fill with the roasty smell of freshly brewed coffee, our first customer was usually standing there patiently, a reusable cup in one hand and stifling a yawn or rubbing sleep from their eyes with the other.

One of my favorite early-morning customers was Jim, a man in his late fifties or early sixties. He always had a big smile and looked like he was headed to a fancy office somewhere with his perfectly pressed white dress shirt, stylish tie, and shiny cuff links. He wore his dark hair slicked back, and he had an easy confidence of success about him. His regular drink was a tall Americano with no room for cream. During the holidays, he'd tip us one hundred dollars by discretely coming to the side of the kiosk, passing us a single bill with a wink, and thanking us for being part of his day.

Stan, an older man in his midseventies with a great sense of humor, was another one of my favorite customers who came in later in the morning. His gray mustache wiggled when he laughed, and he usually wore a *Great Gatsby*–era cap, giving the appearance he was on his way to play golf somewhere. He took great delight in entertaining us and did so often by crafting jokes using the words on the daily coffee-description board.

One day, he sidled up to the register to place his order and noticed that Kenya was the featured coffee of the day. With a twinkle in his eye, he said, "Winey and full bodied, huh? That sounds like my ex-wife." That was Stan.

Our store was fun and fast-paced, and we established a strong base of regular customers in just a few months. As our volume grew, it became evident that more leadership in the store was needed, given that our manager was just part-time. My team members looked to me for guidance and direction, and I often asked for additional responsibility, so I was a natural fit to take up some of the slack.

Eventually, I took over inventory management and filling out a sheet to track the daily sales numbers, revealing to me I liked the business details as much as I liked serving customers.

A lead clerk position was added to the store team to formalize the assumption of these supervisory tasks, and it made sense that this was the next move for me.

I had been a barista for less than six months and already earned my first promotion at Starbucks. I was proud and excited for the added responsibility.

As a twenty-year-old supervisor, I had a great handle on the work and the customers but was a little nervous about providing direction and feedback to the team. We worked well together, but they were all older, and I wasn't sure if they would take direction from me. One of my coworkers, Sue, and I started with Starbucks at the same time, and she was old enough to be my mom. She was a hard worker, extremely efficient, and a little impatient. She'd come back from her smoke breaks and dive into the tasks, sometimes complaining if they hadn't been done while she was gone. I didn't know her background, but she always looked tired, and I had the sense that her life hadn't been easy. Even with our age difference, though, it was clear she respected my authority. Sue had her own ambitions and eventually became a lead clerk herself.

Less than six months into my position, my district manager, Tim, asked if I'd like to be the assistant manager at a new store opening in the Seattle suburb of Bellevue. The promotion was a big deal. It wasn't just because of the job title—it would be my first salaried position ever. When Tim presented the base salary of $17,500/year, it seemed like a lot of money, and that didn't even include the bonus potential if our store hit our sales target. I accepted the offer immediately and went into training to prepare for my first management position.

Two promotions in one year taught me that doing good work and asking to take on more responsibility could lead to bigger and better things—not to mention more money. I had never worked for a company that was big enough to offer me a promotion, and this highly energized me. A fresh wave of motivation kicked into gear, and work suddenly became much more fulfilling than school.

Following my passion and energy instead of the path I was "supposed" to be on, I decided to put my classes on hold. I finally felt that I had a purpose and a future and was motivated and driven to do more, achieve more, and grow more. And I wasn't going to wait until I finished college to figure it out.

The time was now—that much was obvious to me, even if I didn't know exactly where I was going. My career was finally moving forward.

And so was I.

CHAPTER 3

Walking into Starbucks's corporate office took me back to my ten-year-old self. I had dreamed of this day.

On visits to Seattle growing up, I'd stare admiringly at the confident-looking businesswomen striding purposefully along the busy streets of downtown. They were obviously headed somewhere important in their crisp pantsuits with their leather briefcases slung over their shoulders.

I'd watch them walk by, high heels clacking on the pavement with each quick step, and I knew I wanted to be one of them.

I grew up in the interior of Alaska in a small town whose closest city was an eight-hour drive. I didn't see many women dressed like the urbanites of metropolitan Seattle, although I'm sure there were some tucked inside office buildings. The extreme winter temperatures in Fairbanks forced people to cover every inch of their bodies for fear of frostbite. Preferring pragmatism to the discomfort of fashion-forward stilettos, women traded out warm boots for comfortable shoes, clogs, and Rockports once they arrived at the office.

At an early age, I identified more with the cool Seattleites than the hearty Alaskans. It wasn't the fashion I coveted, but the desire to live somewhere bigger and more cosmopolitan. I felt constrained and stifled in Alaska despite its vast geography, almost as if I couldn't breathe fully. Everyone knew everyone else, and you could literally drive from one end of my hometown to the other in less than thirty minutes.

I needed more, and I needed different. I wanted more options and exposure and a bigger world to play in. My goal was independence and self-sufficiency, and that included a job where I could wear pantsuits and high heels.

I always envisioned working in an office. When I was young, my playtime was spent pretending I was at school or an office where I'd situate myself at my bedroom desk. Pencil jar and stapler within reach, I'd prepare fake correspondence with a Publishers Clearing House stamp affixed in the upper right-hand corner as if it were going to the mailbox and then on its way to somewhere important.

In middle school, I worked for my grandma, helping her with various back-office tasks like data entry, photocopying, and filing. She had a consulting business, educating teachers to use computers when they were first introduced into academics.

Administrative work felt important and professional to me. I relished being in the hushed environment, and my senses went into overdrive with the smell of ink from the ditto machine, the whir of the computer, and the sound of shuffling papers. In a weird way, it comforted and soothed me.

I never stopped fantasizing about working in an office since those days with Grandma, and, after a few months as the Bellevue store assistant manager, I decided it was time to find out what was going on at Starbucks corporate.

I grabbed *The Bean Book*—Starbucks's internal telephone directory—and picked up the phone. I wasn't sure whom to call or what to ask, but it was a place to start.

A week later, I walked through the front doors of the corporate office and up the circular stairs to the lobby. I was on my way to meet with Teresa Donich-Harris, an HR employment manager who was doing a lot of the hiring for the company.

I'd been in the corporate office only a couple of times. In fact, I'd hardly been in *any* offices that weren't my dad's or my grandma's. I was excited and nervous with anticipation.

Waiting for Teresa, I noticed two locked double doors flanking either side of the semicircular black Formica front desk. Even though it was fairly quiet and there was no one else in the lobby, I felt an undertone of positive energy. Intrigued, I couldn't wait to see what lay behind the doors and what it took to run the fifty stores Starbucks had amassed by that point.

Suddenly, Teresa pushed through the set of doors on the right with a burst of energy and greeted me warmly, thrusting her hand toward me with a big smile on her face while she introduced herself.

Teresa's attire resembled that of the women I had seen on my visits to Seattle and wistfully wanted to dress like—a plaid wool skirt, crisp white blouse, and black high heels in which she walked impressively fast.

I, in contrast, was just off my shift and still in my uniform. I was more than ready to ditch my comfortable work shoes for an outfit like Teresa's—I had been fantasizing about this since I was a kid.

Teresa said something friendly to the receptionist and thanked her, which put me at ease immediately. I walked behind her as she badged through the double doors, and any intimidation I had entering the front door dissipated.

She guided me to her office, pointing out different departments and people along the way. "There's the Mail Order division. That's the store design team. That's Dave Olsen's office, and there's Howard Schultz's office in the corner looking over the Roasting Plant."

I had heard of these departments and people before but didn't understand what they did and how they contributed to Starbucks. All I knew was my store and some of the other stores in my district. My view of Starbucks was limited to the essential functions of doing my job.

We got some coffee from the break room and sat in her office as she began to ask me a bit about my background and interests. I shared my passion for customer service as well as my hope to get an office job someday.

It turned out that employees from the stores often transitioned into entry-level administration roles at corporate or into the Mail Order division. Store experience was highly valued for these jobs because employees already had a base understanding of the company, the culture, and products offered. It also provided employees a career path out of the stores if growing in operations wasn't right for them.

She paused for a moment and then said, "You know, Chrissy, we actually have an opening for an administrative role in Human Resources. It's a brand-new job and supports the whole team with a variety of projects. It provides some admin support to our vice president, Emily. Would you be interested in learning more about it?"

"Yes, but I have no idea what Human Resources is."

She tipped her head back and laughed and explained that HR was the group that provided programs, tools, and services to make a great employee experience. It consisted of training, recruiting, employee relations, compensation, and benefits. I was most familiar with training because I had been through some of the classes that were offered and helped train new store employees, but I hadn't heard of the other departments before.

There were four people on the team, and they were looking to bring in a coordinator to help with the increased volume of work. The company had almost doubled in size over the previous eighteen months, and there was no sign of slowing down.

At the conclusion of our meeting, Teresa suggested that I would be a good candidate for the job and wanted to have me come in for an interview with Emily. I'm not sure what made me stand out in her mind, but I assumed at the time that it was a combination of my professionalism, store experience, and general curiosity. In hindsight, I think she saw an ambitious twenty-one-year-old who had the courage to make a call to someone she didn't know in hopes that it might lead somewhere. In the end, this would become a major turning point in my career.

I was totally nervous about my upcoming interview with Emily, and, of course, the first thing I worried about was what to wear. I didn't have any business attire at home and didn't have much money to buy anything new, but I knew this was an opportunity to take seriously and I needed to dress the part. I already owned a dark mustard-yellow satiny blazer with thin black-and-white pinstripes, so I bought a black knee-length pencil skirt to go with it. I chose the least coffee-stained white button-down shirt from my barista uniform to wear under my jacket and splurged on my first pair of black pumps. They were fake leather from Payless because I couldn't afford the real deal, and I paired them with a fresh pair of nude pantyhose— bare legs were a no-no in contrast to their acceptance today in the workplace.

With my outfit planned, I turned to preparing for the interview. This didn't take nearly as much time as the clothes because I didn't know much about the job or what it was like to work in an office. But I knew I wanted the job and told myself to remain professional even with the butterflies bouncing off the walls of my stomach.

On the day of my interview, Teresa greeted me in the lobby again and led me back to Emily's office. I had met Emily briefly when Teresa took me on a tour the last time I was there, and I remembered her being very kind, if not a little quiet.

Emily maintained constant eye contact along with a warm smile and moved and talked slowly and tentatively, almost as if she didn't want to frighten me, which was in complete contrast to Teresa's bouncy energy. A bobbed haircut framed her twinkling brown eyes, and she wore a skirt suit and heels.

I would come to learn that Emily's style was more like that of a horse whisperer than a desk pounder. This approach served her well in Starbucks's early days, but eventually the company outgrew her, and future HR leaders became a lot louder to make sure their ideas were heard among all the company priorities.

Emily was very gracious in the interview when she explained that part of the job would require supporting her with administrative tasks. This required a high level of integrity and diplomacy, given the sensitive nature of the issues she dealt with and what I'd be exposed to. In HR, visibility to compensation, employee complaints, and health issues were part of the day-to-day work.

I assured her that I could keep things confidential and could be counted on for discretion. I described a recent situation where I caught a store partner stealing milk because he was broke but needed to feed his family. It was a very uncomfortable situation, but I kept it to myself and my boss, not wanting to embarrass the partner but also treating it like the serious offense that it was.

The last step of my interview with Emily was a typing test where she asked me to type "the quick brown fox jumped over the lazy dog" repeatedly. It seemed silly, but the job required some computer work, and I demonstrated that, though not fast, I was at least proficient enough to do the basics.

A few days later, I was hired as Starbucks's first Human Resources coordinator and the fifth person in the company's HR department.

As I celebrated my third promotion in less than two years and my new office job, I had no idea that Starbucks was on the way to being one of the most respected brands in the world.

I was simply excited to finally become the office worker I dreamed of as a kid.

CHAPTER 4

I took my first corporate job seriously and relished the opportunity to do a little of everything as the Human Resources coordinator.

Even in its early days, Starbucks had a good reputation as an employer that cared about its employees. As a smaller company, we were considered cutting edge with our health insurance coverage for part-time employees, 401(k) with a company match, and robust training and development programs.

My job duties included helping with benefits administration, employment application processing, and maintaining employment records, which required strong attention to detail. The confidential information Emily told me about in my interview was very much a part of my daily work. I was initially surprised about some of the things I was privy to, but eventually learned that it was just part of the job.

My tasks weren't particularly challenging, but learning how to manage the workload and support for team members was. People came to me from different directions with different communication styles, and I navigated prioritizing and managing their expectations. It didn't take long for me to master my own approach to planning and organizing work, a skill that has stayed with me my entire career. I learned to block out time on my calendar for project work and let my team know to avoid interruptions, and I prioritized my tasks each day.

Training and development quickly became my favorite function within HR, in part because of the company training manager, Gay. She taught my coffee class when I was first hired, and I was in awe of her knowledge and her ability to connect with people.

At the time, Gay was the most tenured employee in the entire company, having started in 1979. She was the unofficial Starbucks historian, full of stories and lore about the company's early days.

Her colorful personality and creativity made her stand out in our somewhat subdued office environment. She had an artist's flair with chunky jewelry and stylish glasses, and her red hair was cut in a chic pixie style. When she spoke, she gestured expressively while her bracelets jangled together, and when she smiled, her eyes squinted and her whole face lit up.

I liked working on training tasks and projects because people were usually excited to learn something new. The classroom was considered a positive environment of collaboration and open-mindedness and provided participants a break from their daily job activities and normal work teams.

Everyone who was hired to work in Starbucks stores cycled through the office for training on customer service, barista skills, merchandise, and extensive coffee knowledge.

Baristas were expected to be able to taste, describe, and recommend a varietal or blend of coffee based on the customer's preferences. They were instructed to keep a brochure called *The World of Coffee* in their apron pocket should a customer ask a question they didn't know the answer to. They'd deftly pull it out, lay it on the counter, and point to some interesting fact to impress them with how much they knew.

Back then, Starbucks was the ultimate coffee authority, and training was apportioned accordingly. Thirty percent of training time was spent on coffee knowledge and the remaining on everything else. Given that you couldn't find a decaf soy grande caramel Frappuccino with extra caramel anywhere at that time, knowledge about coffee varietals and blends was the top priority. The stores didn't have blenders yet, and espresso beverages were limited to hot or iced, whole milk or 2 percent. That was it.

Today's more complex beverage offerings, warmed food, and stringent operational processes and standards leave little time for coffee knowledge in barista training. Much of it is done on the job in the form of coffee tastings, often spearheaded by an enthusiastic barista on the quest toward Coffee Master status.

As the Human Resources coordinator, I helped Gay track training participants, create the class schedules, and print completion certificates for attendees.

I eventually noticed that the class offerings and training structure for new retail employees were very robust but lacking for nonretail employees. Hiring at the office was happening at an equally rapid pace, and, given the growth, I felt this was a big miss.

I believed that an inconsistent indoctrination into the company history, culture, and values put our mission at risk and that baseline coffee knowledge and barista skills were an essential part of being a Starbucks employee. It didn't matter whether you worked in the stores or not—all employees should be able to at least describe and recommend coffees to friends and family members and make themselves a high-quality latte. I firmly believed we all had a stake in our mission: to establish Starbucks as the premier purveyor of the finest coffee in the world while maintaining our uncompromising principles as we grew.

I asked Emily and Gay if I could take a stab at putting together an onboarding curriculum for new nonretail hires, and when no one else raised their hand to be the classroom trainer, I volunteered for that too.

I was always looking for ways to make things better and putting structure and order in places where there wasn't any, a personality trait that was a part of me since I was a kid. I loved making sense of a disorganized kitchen cabinet and once even cleaned out my uncle's closet to get rid of all the clothes that were either out of style or no longer fit him.

My skills were ripe for tackling the inconsistency in how office and warehouse employees were trained, and even though I didn't have any experience, my passion for the idea gave me the confidence that I could figure it out with some help.

Gay created a development plan for me that included teaching classes so she could observe me and provide feedback. She taught me how to modify the barista training materials to meet the needs of our nonretail participants, and I was up and teaching my first class in just a couple of weeks.

At first, I followed the facilitator guide to a T, afraid to miss any important content. But in time, I became more comfortable with the flow and relaxed into my own style. I learned how to key into the specific needs of the group, picking up on their cues and questions with more astuteness. My listening skills became highly refined, and I became adept at flexing the training outline while still accomplishing the goals.

The original proposal to take on the additional responsibility didn't account for the increase in the rest of my work volume that came with the company's growth. Eventually, I requested to hire a part-time file clerk to help me so I could focus on the more complex areas of my job. The job I was originally hired for had expanded, and I was growing right along with it.

I knew I was making an impact on the future of Starbucks, although I didn't know to what extent at the time. The work I did in training and development to instill Starbucks's mission and values in all nonretail employees set the standard for how it's done today—for over two hundred thousand employees across the globe.

After the new training-class schedule was rolling for a few months with orientation and coffee-knowledge classes, I realized that there was a gap in the ability of our employees to prepare quality beverages outside of the classroom. My training courses taught them the skills, but they didn't have a way to practice. The office and warehouse kitchens didn't stock the same equipment or coffee-making accoutrements as in the training classroom or in the stores. This seemed incongruent to me, given that we were a coffee company serving the finest coffee in the world, and yet you couldn't find a great cup in the office unless you happened to brew up a French press.

I shared this observation with Emily, and she suggested I make a proposal of what should be in the kitchens and how much it would cost. This type of project was completely new to me, but it was another one of those situations I'd have to figure out by doing. There's a first time for everything, especially when you're early in your career.

After a couple of weeks of research and calculations, I presented my proposal to Emily. She thought it looked good but told me I needed to present it to Orin Smith, the then cfo of Starbucks. My first thought was what a big deal it was to meet with him. I was surprised that he would meet to review such a nominal expense, but, in retrospect, I think Emily arranged this for my development.

I didn't know much about Orin or what a cfo did except that I knew he was an important man. He came to Starbucks a year after I started and was the company's first cfo. He would later serve as ceo from 2000 to 2005.

Orin was friendly and smiled at me when I walked by in the hallway, but we'd never said more than a few words to one another before. He looked older than my father with his salt-and-pepper hair, and he was one of the few people who wore a suit jacket to the office each day. He was often there before me as evidenced by his dated brown four-door sedan in its usual parking spot in front of the building.

I was a little nervous about my meeting with him, in part because of his positional power, but it was also my first time ever requesting that the company spend money on a project I was working on.

I showed up at his office a few minutes early and chatted with his assistant while I waited. His door was closed, but I could see him through the window, talking with someone who was sitting across his desk from him. Orin leaned forward and nodded occasionally before he said anything in return, as though absorbing the words of the person in front of him. He carried himself with a calm demeanor, and I could tell that he was a thoughtful listener, giving those he spoke with his full attention.

When it was my turn to go into his office, he stood up and smiled and then spoke first.

"Hi, Chrissy. Emily tells me that you've been working on a proposal to upgrade the coffee station in the kitchen. What have you got?"

I was a little surprised at how quickly he got to the point, but I was confident in my recommendation. I was well pre-pared with the initial and ongoing costs and had written a few notes about why this project was important.

I pushed a crude spreadsheet toward him and spoke. "Here are the start-up and ongoing costs. But this isn't just about money. Investing in the kitchen is an important part of the employee experience. By having the same supplies and equip-ment available to nonretail employees, it connects us to our mission of having the highest-quality coffee."

Twenty-two-year-old Chrissy Parr had just delivered her first business case.

A smile bloomed on his face. "I agree. But it still has a cost we need to plan for. Walk me through the alternatives you considered."

Unbeknownst to me, I was getting business coaching by one of the top leaders in the company, which would serve me well decades later in my career.

After I walked him through the options, he approved my leading recommendation without hesitation and thanked me for my work and for caring about the employee experience. I floated out of his office, stoked that I had his approval but even more thrilled that I was going to give my coworkers what they deserved.

Thirty days later, when the kitchen was fully furnished and brimming with coffee-making supplies and ingredients, I hosted a ribbon-cutting ceremony and milk-foaming competition, complete with chocolate medals for participants.

To this day, you won't find a Starbucks office in the world without at least one coffee-making kitchen complete with espresso machines and a Frappuccino station. I had unknowingly created a cultural and workplace standard that would extend globally and live beyond my Starbucks tenure.

* * *

Exposure to senior executives like Orin was one of the perks of being in HR at a small company. I respected their experience and became a keen observer of the personalities, work styles, and roles of the most senior executives in the company through daily interaction. Their business minds intrigued me, and I considered it an opportunity to learn from them and absorb whatever I could.

Dave Olsen, at that time the vice president of Coffee, was easygoing and laughed a lot. When he wasn't visiting origin countries, he spent most of his time in the coffee-tasting room, sampling offerings that came from all over the world. I learned later that Dave had founded Cafe Allegro, the espresso bar where I had my first caffè mocha when I was a receptionist at the hair salon in the University District.

Down the hall was Lawrence Maltz, the suave head of business development. His job was a mystery to me, but I often saw him meeting with other senior executives, and he seemed to have a lot of relationships with colleagues outside of the office. He walked the halls, looking sophisticated and confident in his cashmere sweaters and Italian shoes, his full head of hair thick and silvery.

Jack Rodgers was around the corner from me, worked part-time, and was always superfriendly when I ran into him in the corridor. He had the look of a grandpa with his white hair and was usually wearing some sort of sweater with his slacks. When he greeted me in the hall, he'd stop me, grab my hands, look right into my eyes, and say, "Chrissy, how are you?" He seemed genuinely interested in my response and always spent a few minutes talking with me. I didn't understand what he did either, but I knew he was an important adviser to Howard and the board. I later learned he was one of the original investors in Starbucks.

Howard Schultz's office was next to Orin's and overlooked the Roasting Plant where all coffee was roasted, packaged, and boxed up to go to the stores and wholesale accounts. I'm pretty sure he chose this location not to monitor what was going on below but to connect him to the company's core—the coffee and the people creating it. You seldom found Howard in his office anyway, because he was always walking around, talking with employees and department leaders. He was filled with a pent-up passionate energy and curiosity, which made it hard for him to sit still. Employees never seemed intimidated by his presence but fed off it, as it gave people purpose to their work if he showed an inkling of interest.

We were a small company with big ambitions, and the energy was nonstop. I didn't know much about what was being discussed in the meetings I wasn't a part of, but it all felt like we had the same shared mission to expand the Starbucks experience. We were moving forward with intensity, destined to create something great.

* * *

About a year after I moved into Human Resources, I was told confidentially that the company was preparing for its initial public offering. I didn't know what that meant exactly, but I could tell from the way Emily and our benefits manager, Bradley, were acting that this was a very big deal.

To celebrate this huge company milestone, local employees were invited to attend an event at the Roasting Plant for a special announcement. There were no specifics about what the gathering was for, but speculation ran high and wide.

Burlap bags filled with unroasted coffee had been pushed to the sides and rows of plastic chairs set in their place. The burned-toast smell of the latest batch of roasted coffee still lingered in the air, and a small stage of sorts had been established on one end of the plant floor.

When employees walked in, they were handed a glass of sparkling cider while jazz music played in the background.

Howard stepped up to the mic and asked everyone to take a seat. The room quieted with anticipation.

After he thanked everyone for coming, he proceeded to passionately share his vision for the company that had been born on a trip to Milan, Italy, many years prior. He spoke about founding Il Giornale in 1986 to bring the romance of the

Italian stand-up coffee bar to the United States and of why he bought Starbucks in 1987.

He expressed his deep appreciation for all the Starbucks employees who had been part of the journey up to that point and affirmed that he wanted to create a different kind of company for them. He excitedly shared that there were so many communities that had not yet benefited from the Starbucks experience, and there were more people to reach. He reminded us that the ambitions for Starbucks were focused on large and global company growth.

And then came the moment everyone was waiting for to find out whether the rumors were true. Howard announced that Starbucks was going public, and employees would benefit from a new stock-option program called Bean Stock. We were no longer employees; we were now all "partners" in the company. Partners in growth.

This was revolutionary in the early nineties as the only other companies that were providing stock options to employees were early-stage technology companies. Every Starbucks employee who worked more than twenty hours per week was provided a personalized statement of their first stock-option grant tucked in a folder that I had hand tied with a blue satin ribbon.

The room roared with applause and enthusiastic cheers as we hugged one another, sparkling cider sloshing out of our plastic champagne glasses. It was a significant moment in the company's history and in the lives of those of us that were a part of it.

Going public put everything into hyperdrive.

Not long after the IPO, we grew out of our offices, and the Seattle Roasting Plant was bursting at the seams. Starbucks had over one hundred stores at that point with plans for thousands more. Another roasting plant was built south of Seattle as a pressure-release valve and in anticipation of future needs.

In 1993, the corporate offices started to migrate to a building a few blocks away. It was an old brick building with over two million square feet of hardwood floors that used to be the national distribution center for the Sears catalog. Known by Starbucks partners as the Starbucks Support Center (SCC), the company's world headquarters is still there today.

The HR department was one of the first groups to move, and I was excited to be in our new space on the eighth floor.

The building hadn't been completely redone yet, and we were reliant on the cafeteria on the third floor to host large group gatherings because there was no other space to do so. It was an old-school deli with blue-and-white decor, hard plastic chairs, and institutional-style tables. The big concrete columns every ten feet made it less than ideal for meetings, but it was our only option at the time. There was no food service or fancy technology because we were watching every penny to ensure money went back into store growth.

The all-employee meetings, dubbed "open forums," fell under my responsibility and were becoming more frequent due to Howard's desire to maintain a level of transparency with partners during the rapid growth. Communication was key to keeping people informed and feeling part of all that was going on.

At one such convening, we gathered for a special surprise announcement. I decided to rent the best TV/VCR combo unit our department could afford for the accompanying video, even though either multiple screens or a much larger single screen was needed for all two hundred attendees to get a good view. But it was what we had, and it would have to do.

After our customary coffee tasting, Howard addressed the group. He was his usual charismatic, passionate self, speaking without a script. He was a fantastic storyteller and could enrapture and inspire any audience but especially Starbucks partners. People hung on his every word when he spoke and took what he said to heart and personally.

When it was time to queue the video, I jumped into position to flip it on. Howard looked toward the TV/VCR unit, dumbfounded. The smile fell off his face. He glanced down at the ground for a millisecond and then shook his head. "This is it?" he said, looking right at me.

I nodded.

"That won't work. No one will be able to see it or hear it," he responded.

He turned to the audience and apologized for the inadequate setup and told them that we'd find another way to get them the video.

My face flushed with embarrassment, and I tried to keep from bursting into tears. I said nothing and retreated toward the back of the room. I knew he was right—the video equipment was totally inadequate. I had accepted the budget we had and figured I needed to make do with it versus pressing for what I knew was right.

I was so worked up after the open forum that I decided to send Howard an email.

I wanted him to know how I felt about the whole situation, from the decision to rent the TV/VCR unit to how I felt shamed in front of everyone when he said it wouldn't work. I was trying to do my best, and my best wasn't good enough.

After I drafted the email, I hemmed and hawed for a few minutes, trying to decide if I should push Send. I mean, would this go anywhere? Would I get fired for the video debacle or for telling him how I felt about it?

I realized I didn't care. I felt so strongly that I had made the best decision I could, given the circumstances, and didn't think I should be penalized for it.

I clicked the mouse and waited to see what might come of it.

An hour later, a reply from Howard popped up in my inbox asking me to come to his office. I was surprised that he read my message so quickly and even more surprised that he didn't have his assistant reach out to me to schedule a meeting. He was asking me to come as soon as I could. I realized I must have hit a nerve.

I had no idea what to expect when I walked toward his office door, my palms moist in anticipation and my shirt turning damp with sweat.

When I saw his face, I exhaled with relief. He looked unsettled but not angry.

He said he was genuinely concerned that I was upset by the situation, and he wanted to understand how he could help partners at my level be empowered to make the right decisions. Bureaucracy confounded and frustrated him. It wasn't about me making a bad decision; it was about his disappointment in the whole system. He wanted a culture of trust and nimbleness, not constraints.

I thanked him for listening to me and seeking to understand my frustrations. I felt he cared, and change would come of this.

I took a risk by pressing Send on that email, but I learned a powerful lesson: if you don't speak up, nothing will change.

Exposure to leaders like Orin and Howard so early in my career made an indelible impact on me. No one discouraged me from speaking up or taking the initiative to improve a process or solve a problem, so I kept doing it. I got an adrenaline boost when I took on more responsibility and felt like I was making an impact.

While I didn't leave the stores with my sights set on human resources and training as a career path, I never would have known if I hadn't taken the initiative and picked up *The Bean Book* to make that first call to see what jobs might be available at Starbucks corporate.

I learned during these early stages of my career that if I don't ask, nothing will just magically appear. New opportunities, additional resources, and more responsibility all came when I put myself out there. And they still do to this day.

CHAPTER 5

As a kid, I couldn't wait to be a grown-up. Being an adult was going to be so awesome and freeing—no one to tell me what to do. I'd be able to eat whatever I wanted, go to bed when I wanted, and skip brushing my teeth if I wanted.

What no one told me was that being a grown-up would be hard.

Sure, I could see it in the faces or hear it in the voices of the adults around me that adulthood wasn't all sunshine and ponies. I saw my dad, a single parent, come home from work, exhausted, and then have to figure out what relatively nutritious meal he could cobble together for my brother and me, trying to shut out our bickering while he cooked.

As much as I coveted independence from a very young age, becoming a self-sufficient young woman meant learning from life's mistakes like bank account overdrafts and missed credit card payments. When I was twenty and working at a toy store downtown to earn some extra holiday cash, I didn't show up one day because I was too hungover and got fired as a result. At age twenty-two, I left my car at a repair shop, and when I picked it up the next day, the whole driver's side was bashed in. They said I had brought it in that way. I had no proof that it happened under their watch and was totally taken advantage of—and had no savings to buy a replacement vehicle.

Growing up was hard. I was no longer protected by the innocence and naivete of youth—I was on my own.

I learned from these lessons, but, as I got older, it seemed the stakes got higher and the pressures and stresses became weightier. I moved beyond mastering basic life skills like banking, holding down a job, and managing a budget to learning how to navigate highly complex life problems.

And life doled out two big ones when I least expected it.

I was having fun at my job at Starbucks because there was so much going on all the time. The pace in the newly renamed Partner Resources department picked up dramatically after the initial public offering. It seemed like there was a weekly announcement of some major initiative—the first stock split, the first drive-through store, the introduction of a new beverage. Two years after Starbucks went public, the number of stores had doubled, and there was no slowdown in sight.

In some ways, I was ahead of other people in their early twenties because I dropped out of college. I could focus 100 percent on my career instead of burying myself in boring textbooks or sitting in a large lecture hall and letting useless knowledge wash over me.

My small salary was stretched, but it was just enough to rent my first apartment by myself, a tiny studio in a brick building on a busy street in Seattle's Eastlake neighborhood. I was financially independent, owned a fully paid-for Ford Escort, and had no debt except a small credit card balance at Macy's.

I worked nights at a local bar, pouring beer and wine to make some extra cash that funded things like a trip to Club Med in Mexico and going out with friends.

Along the way, I met my husband, Tate, and he exposed me to Seattle's outdoor offerings, which filled our weekends. Activities like hiking and skiing soon became things we shared together frequently. Eventually, I quit my bartending job, and we moved in together, getting married a year later.

I had a good job, a life partner, and a nice group of friends, but things were not all they appeared to be on the outside. While I was physically and mentally healthy and looked like I had it all together, my mom was not.

My mom had always had mental health issues; I just didn't know to what degree until I got older. She had left my brother, Jason, and me with our dad when we were very young because she was not prepared to parent two young kids at the age of twenty-one.

Jason and I visited her in Seattle on occasion when we were kids. We were curious about her colorful group of friends, and we enjoyed being exposed to the vibrancy and diversity of Seattle at a very young age.

The only glimmer of potential mental health issues back then was that she was always switching jobs or starting up some new hobby. I'm sure there were earlier signs, but I just didn't see or understand them. Her jobs and hobbies were wide reaching—from breeding potbellied pigs, to starting her espresso cart business, to working in construction, or at a nursery. The only thing constant with my mom was change.

Whatever she took on was done with intense exuberance and passion. Everything else would be cast aside while she became singularly focused. Inevitably, her high level of enthusiasm would gradually fade when the newness wore off, or a challenge threw her for a loop—either with the endeavor itself or with another personality involved. When I was younger, I thought it was a sign of creativity that she never settled into anything for very long, but I eventually learned it was a tell of something more.

As I got older, her behavior became more erratic. She started having a hard time holding down a job and an even harder time finding supportive and healthy relationships.

Extreme bouts of emotional stress peppered with substance abuse swelled into an ongoing mental health crisis that I was absolutely not prepared to handle in my midtwenties.

Her unpredictability had me strapped into the seat of a fast-moving emotional roller coaster, and I couldn't figure out how to get off, or at least slow it down. I was continually on edge because I never knew what the next phone call would bring.

The incidents that invariably pulled me in were not always the same, but the behavior patterns were consistent. After a long quiet period, something would trigger her (usually an interpersonal conflict), and then she would isolate herself. If it was really bad, she would become self-destructive.

Tate got exposed to all of it when we were dating, and he unquestioningly supported both me and my mom, while he and I were also trying to get our footing on our own responsibilities of adulthood. Every day, a ringing phone could mean a call for help from my mom, struggling to come up from the depths of a low point. Even worse, the police, a hospital, or one of her concerned friends might be on the other end of the line, and the day would be turned upside down by a trip to the emergency room to check on her.

I wasn't prepared for the reversal of roles in our parent-child relationship, and it caused an incredible amount of stress and chaos in my life, which I tried hard to keep out of the workplace. At times, I felt my life was being held together with a very fine thread that was gradually unraveling, and I did everything I could to keep the frayed ends from becoming even looser.

When Tate and I got engaged, wedding planning provided a nice distraction from the tumult with my mom. We were excited to host our family in Seattle and leveraged all the Pacific Northwest had to offer.

Our rehearsal dinner was to be held at the Space Needle, and our ceremony and reception were to take place in a quintessentially Seattle brick building in the Pioneer Square neighborhood. Because many of our relatives would be traveling from out of state, the wedding would be as much a family reunion as a celebration of our marriage.

A week before the wedding, I telephoned my family members to make sure they had all the details and to see if they needed anything. My last call was to my mom because a small part of me worried that things had been too calm of late. I knew that being around so many family members and in big social situations could be overwhelming for her, and this weighed on me in anticipation of our wedding day. I made sure that her role in the festivities was low pressure and behind the scenes, but, as mother of the bride, she would be unable to hide completely.

I made the check-in call to her while I was at work from a private conference room across the building from my office.

I dialed her home number. She picked up on the third ring.

"Hello?" Her voice was somewhat gravelly from years of smoking.

"Hi, Mom. It's Chris. How are you?"

"I'm okay." I could immediately tell she wasn't. Her voice was tentative and somewhat meek. I pictured her on the other end of the phone, holding on to a cup of coffee with shaky hands.

"I wanted to check in about the wedding events this week and to see if you had any questions or needed anything." Deep down I was anxious. She had been pretty quiet the last few weeks, and I wasn't sure why.

"Um, I need to tell you that I can't go. I'm not up for it. I think it's more than I can handle right now."

I was stunned and hurt. Nothing was more important to me than having her there. I didn't think I was asking for much. I was planning on getting married only once in my life, and she couldn't handle it for an hour or two? Her emotional fragility felt like an unreasonable excuse. As upset as I was, I had known deep down this might happen. I had just hoped it wouldn't.

I hung up the phone, shaking and trying to keep the tears at bay. I lingered in the conference room, trying to pull myself together before I went back to my desk to face my coworkers. I didn't want anyone to see me upset. Tears pooled at the corners of my eyes, and I used my sleeve to wipe away my smeared mascara.

After a few deep breaths, I exited the conference room and went back to my work area to focus on the tasks at hand. I'm sure people working near me could sense that something was up, but I kept my head down and didn't engage with anyone. I felt all alone.

After the wedding, I decided to open up to my boss, Joan, about the stress my mom's mental health was causing me. It was starting to wear on me, and, although Joan never said anything about my performance, I could feel the strain it put on my work—not in quality, but in my energy and attentiveness. Joan listened with kindness. She was empathetic and helped me understand that pretty much everyone has something they are dealing with outside of work.

Joan's care and patience taught me not just how to show compassion for my team members when I became a leader but how to give myself grace. As I took on more responsibility, I put more pressure on myself to succeed, and Joan's guidance and support while I navigated my mom's struggle with mental health were a constant reminder that I could get through anything.

Watching my mom struggle and bounce from one thing to another taught me to approach things in a completely different manner. I was determined to be not just a survivor but a *thriver.* I set big goals and then, like a terrier, hold on and don't give up until I've achieved them. I covet new challenges especially when I have a stable platform to support me while I'm going after them.

My second big lesson of being an adult presented itself not long after Tate and I got married.

I was still in Partner Resources but had moved into the training department full-time. My job provided me good perspective and breadth on all the happenings within the company because I worked on training programs for the corporate office and the roasting plants.

Innovation and growth were happening at a very rapid pace throughout the company. Frappuccino Blended Beverage was added to the menu boards as the first new beverage platform since I'd become a partner. It was born out of an experiment by a store manager in California seeking to offer her customers a product they were asking for—something sweet, creamy, and cold to beat the heat.

One group I worked with was a small but passionate team called Specialty Sales and Marketing, or SS&M for short.

SS&M sold wholesale Starbucks coffee to restaurants, food-service businesses, hotels, Costco, and any place that proclaimed, "We Proudly Brew Starbucks." This side of the business was growing faster than the retail stores, and I was responsible for creating training and development programs for SS&M team members in addition to coffee-quality programs for their wholesale customers.

My role embedded me in their department, and I found the group to be highly energetic and fun to work with. I hadn't been around salespeople before, and their gregarious, extroverted nature helped pull me out of my introverted shell.

I worked on a training program for one of SS&M's biggest accounts, ITT Sheraton Hotels. As part of the coffee program for Sheraton, Starbucks agreed to customize training materials to ensure the kitchen, room-service, and banquet staff had training to ensure the highest level of Starbucks coffee quality in the hotels. It was an exciting project and one of the first I owned in my new role as training manager.

While working on the ITT Sheraton project, I met Tom, one of the sales managers in the group, who was stationed in Portland.

Tom had been in sales for many years and really loved the people side of the business, especially his team. Nothing brought Tom more joy than having his direct reports over for a meal. With an American mom and a Mexican dad, he was equally as likely to fire up the barbecue as he was to serve homemade tamales.

Growing up in northern California and attending Humboldt State University left its mark on Tom. Even though he mastered the ability to dress like a yuppie in pressed slacks and button-down dress shirts at work, his hippie roots showed outside the office when he wore Birkenstocks long before they were cool.

As a leader, Tom was driven and results-oriented yet highly relational and sometimes even overly emotional. He listened intently and demonstrated a deep level of caring for those he worked with. He wore his heart on his sleeve, sometimes to a fault when he took things too personally.

When he was confused, his whole face wrinkled up, and when he "got it," his face would relax. He'd tilt his head back a bit while nodding slightly as a smile emerged.

Tom never made things about his ego or his agenda. He clearly invested in the success of those who worked for him without an eye on personal accolades. He put people first. He defined what it means to be a servant leader.

Tom was generous with his time and freely shared his knowledge of the business with me while I supported SS&M. He eagerly brought me into the fold by inviting me to meetings with his team and customers and shared business documents and information with me openly and enthusiastically.

I wanted to learn as much about the business as possible so I could better serve the SS&M team with more-relevant programs, and Tom was more than willing to help me. He became an instant role model for me and significantly shaped my leadership style to this day.

After I worked with SS&M for about six months, Tom asked me to come to Portland with his team for a sales retreat. I had never been on a business trip, and I was excited and nervous at the same time. I was going with the cool kids, and I wanted to fit in but also make sure that I delivered value. He asked for my help facilitating a workshop, and that certainly fell within my job description, so I was all in.

I learned so much about the business on that trip, and it helped me realize that I no longer wanted to be in a support function—I wanted to be in the action, not on the sidelines. I wanted more than ever to be a part of what they were doing—bringing the Starbucks experience to locations outside of the core retail stores.

Never in my life had I envisioned myself in a sales role until that retreat. I am an introvert. I don't like schmoozing people and am not comfortable negotiating. I am more at ease on the outside of the circle, observing what is happening around me and connecting with others one-on-one. I like being around other people but don't like to draw attention to myself. And, I perceived that all salespeople were flashy and had big personalities, which is not at all how I'd describe myself.

But the group from the Portland retreat showed me that not everyone needed to fit the stereotypical salesperson mold to succeed in a sales role.

I loved the camaraderie of the team members and how they were competitive but not in a cutthroat kind of way. Instead, they motivated one another and celebrated each other's accomplishments with genuine enthusiasm.

As I watched them engage, the thought of trying sales still scared the crap out of me, but I realized that fear meant more reason to try. Pushing myself outside my comfort zone was what I needed.

Plus, the idea of being out in the field instead of in an office, meeting with different business owners on their turf, and helping them make great coffee looked fun and challenging.

The more I thought about it, the more I wanted to give it a shot. After all, what was the worst thing that could happen? I knew I'd still have a job somewhere at Starbucks, and at least I showed that I was willing to try something new. It was possible I could totally fail or, an even crazier thought, I could knock it out of the park and have a whole new career ahead of me.

Whatever came of it was meant to be. I was ready for a change, and I had Tom's complete support as my mentor.

I broached the idea of going into a sales role with my boss in the training department, and she was also very supportive. She was a fan of cross-functional moves, so we worked together to create a formal development plan to move me into SS&M for one year as a rotational assignment, at which point I'd be promoted to a director in training and development. The enhanced business knowledge I'd get working in SS&M meant that I could apply that acumen in training and when working with business leaders. It would help me relate and solve problems for them in new ways.

It was very unconventional to go from a corporate staff position to a field position without any previous experience. But my boss, Tom, and I were all committed to doing what it took to make it happen.

Tom had been recruiting me for months at this point, so when I shared my draft development plan with him, he looked at me with a big grin on his face. "So, when do we get started?" he asked.

He told me that that one of the reasons he invited me to Portland was because he had seen me build strong relationships in an approachable manner with his team, and he was confident I could do that well with customers. He said that, as a trainer, I was motivational and demonstrated command. He had a feeling I'd be good in a sales role because of these traits. I was grateful for his enthusiastic support, and his belief in me gave me an extra dose of assurance.

He suggested we formalize our mentoring relationship and put some more structure behind it. He assigned me one of his territories in California as a case study to learn from. It was in the Los Angeles area, and the team consisted of five salespeople, plus a relatively experienced manager who had come to the company with a background in food and beverage sales. The market was positioned for a high level of growth, yet also faced stiff competition from institutional coffee companies selling cheap coffee in bulk (like Sara Lee and Community Coffee) as well as boutique retailers like the Coffee Bean & Tea Leaf.

Tom and I set up biweekly meetings to walk through different elements of the business. He was a patient teacher and tapped into my curiosity by asking me questions to get my perspective. He probed into what decisions I might make if I were the sales manager responsible for the territory and how I would handle people issues.

After working with Tom for several months, I became more and more excited about the idea of working on his team. Any niggling fears or insecurities about an impending transition were overridden by the anticipation of trying something completely new.

Soon enough, an account manager role covering the downtown Seattle territory came available. Of course, there was still so much more to learn, but there was no time like the present. If I didn't take this job, who knew when the next position would open. It was a small team, and there wasn't a lot of turn-over in the Seattle market.

There were about a hundred accounts in the territory, many of them high-profile restaurants, as well as some hotels, corporate offices, and a couple of in-city colleges. It was a prime territory because there was good exposure from a brand perspective and Starbucks executives dined at many of the accounts, which meant additional visibility for me. Another benefit was the compact nature of the territory that made it easy to visit several accounts in a day by walking while my car stayed parked in one spot.

The account base had experienced a business decline over the past twelve months, and Tom said that they needed a different approach and style—someone with humility, per-sistence, and exceptional follow-up. I may not have felt com-pletely ready, but he felt that the market was ready for me. I accepted the position and was stoked to start my career as a sales professional.

While I was excited for the new role, not everyone around me understood why I was making this transition.

Some of my new colleagues in SS&M were curious because they perceived the change as a demotion. I was moving into a less visible, noncorporate role where the career path didn't usually lend itself to cross-functional moves. I knew that it was the right move for me—the rotation would help me become a more well-rounded businessperson.

I also dealt with opinions from other partners in the office who viewed SS&M as a bit of a rogue business unit—mavericks driven by a sale, regardless of brand fit or an account's abil-ity to hold up the coffee-quality standards. I didn't care. I was more than excited about my new job and team.

The retail stores were the darling and where the long-term growth was, and, by going into SS&M, I was, in a sense, switching majors, at least temporarily. But I knew this wasn't a forever decision. It was a for-right-now decision.

I had Tate's total support for the new job even though we had our plates plenty full of change in other areas of our life.

We had bought our first home, a nine-hundred-square-foot 1930s farmhouse in Seattle's Magnolia neighborhood. We were excited to be first-time homeowners and spent every weekend in the garden, experimenting with different plants after seeking counsel from Tate's grandparents, who were both Master Gardeners.

And, as if my new job, new house, and a recently adopted shelter dog weren't enough change, Tate decided to quit his office job to start his own business buying homes and fixing them up to sell. He was happy to be unchained from a desk and to dive into his passion of remodeling homes, capitalizing on the hot Seattle real estate market. This meant he wouldn't have a steady monthly salary, but hopefully a big check would come in when a project sold. We weren't sure exactly how it was all going to work out, and I was a little nervous about how this might impact our financial situation, but I had faith in him and his vision.

It was a chaotic time, but I knew it would work itself out and we'd find a way through it.

I plunged myself into learning as much as I could about sales and quickly realized that it could be a lot of fun but required a different sort of self-motivation. Most of my days were spent alone or with my accounts, and I didn't have much interaction with my peers other than at our Monday-morning business meeting.

There was also much more focus on numbers and business metrics than when I was in training. We all had targets, and I welcomed the accountability—it was one of the reasons I wanted the assignment. I was craving tangible goals that I could directly connect to the department's financial performance.

I paid careful attention to those who consistently hit or exceeded their numbers to see what they were doing and how they were doing it. I read every sales book, went to classes, and took to heart the coaching my boss, Doug, gave me. I wanted to crush the one-year rotational assignment before I went back into the training department. I wanted to show others what was possible.

As Tom suspected, my strength in building relationships and a strong desire to help others turned me into a good salesperson. My excellent follow-up skills and hyperorganized nature lent themselves well to putting together growth plans with my customers. I was surprised by my success because I thought sales required that certain type of extroverted personality I saw on TV.

But the pressure I put on myself to not just *meet* expectations but to *exceed* them grew. In my mind, if Tom and the rest of the SS&M team were going to take a chance on me by putting an inexperienced salesperson in one of the most visible territories in the company, there was no way I was going to let them down.

What started out as an appropriate level of stress for a new job progressively intensified and turned into bouts of anxiety. Even though the pressure came from me, not my managers, it was very real and beginning to cause problems.

The anxiety led to insomnia, and being tired all the time made it hard to concentrate. I'd forget the little things that normally I'd be on top of. I didn't want to socialize as much, and the lack of sleep made me edgy. After a couple of months, my coworkers started to become concerned about my health and well-being because I looked pale and had dark circles under my eyes. I wasn't myself.

Either this made its way back to Tom or he could see for himself, because one day he asked if we could go out to lunch to catch up. He wasn't my direct boss, so I knew something was up.

After we ordered, he opened the conversation with a polite inquiry about what Tate and I had been up to recently. A few minutes later, he shifted the focus and looked at me with deep concern in his eyes. I was running on fumes with three consecutive nights of pretty much zero sleep.

"Hey, Christine. I wanted to have lunch with you today to see how you're doing. I'm worried about you and care about you."

"I'm okay. I just haven't been able to sleep much. I think I'm putting pressure on myself in this job. I know I just started, but I want to do well. Really well. I think about the numbers all the time."

A slow, compassionate smile spread across his face.

"Christine, you're doing great. We're all talking about how quickly you've gotten up to speed, and you've had some great wins. The team loves you, and so do our customers. You're being too hard on yourself," he said.

"Really?" I replied, poking at my salad.

"Yes. Cut yourself some slack. We all care about you and want you to be successful. We've got your back. You're doing great."

I looked up, tears rolling down my cheeks. His kindness overwhelmed me. Here I was, questioning if I was cut out for sales, and Tom was saying nothing of the sort. In fact, he had just said quite the opposite. The fear of failure and self-doubt was all in my head. I was putting an inordinate amount of pressure on myself, and it was killing me.

I'm not sure what made me think I needed to be the top-performing account manager after just a couple of months in the role. Perhaps it was the terrier in me holding on with all my might to show others that this was a good decision, or maybe it was my natural desire to perform well. Deep down, I think it was because I've always been afraid of disappointing people who have invested in me.

With Tom's affirmation, I gently reminded myself why I made this big career change in the first place—to grow and stretch myself, which, unbeknownst to me, also meant learning how to manage my stress.

After my lunch with Tom, I went to the doctor to get myself sorted out. I took prescription sleeping pills for a short stint to help me get back on track. I knew they weren't a sustainable solution, but they certainly helped me start to feel normal.

I decided to join a gym even though I'd never been much of an exerciser, because I couldn't think of any other way to manage my stress. A lot of my SS&M colleagues were runners, and I heard that physical activity could help people expend energy, blow off steam, and sleep better. It was worth a try.

With my new gym routine established, it didn't take long for me to feel back to my normal self. Exercising cleared my mind, and I learned to release some of the pressure I put on myself. I started sleeping through the night, and my mood and confidence improved.

As hard as it was, the lesson was valuable to me in so many ways. I was undoubtedly going to be faced with work-related pressures again in my career, and finding ways to manage them without letting them destroy me was critical. At the ripe old age of twenty-seven, I learned that physical and mental self-care were keys to success.

My time in SS&M ended up becoming a major part of my Starbucks history—what was intended to be a one-year assignment ended up turning into a seven-year career. I was promoted four times during my tenure in SS&M and eventually had a territory that included all business west of the Mississippi River with team members scattered across the western half of the US.

Learning how to deal with my mom's mental health issues as well as my own helped me become the adult I always wanted to be—resourceful, self-sufficient, and independent. Early adulthood was about developing productive coping mechanisms, leaning on the support of others, and learning how to practice self-care.

I became a better manager and leader as a result of my own hardships. I became attuned to what members of my team were dealing with and sought ways to support them, much like Joan and Tom did for me. I was compassionate toward their personal circumstances and tried to be flexible and understanding.

I was growing up. At work and in life.

CHAPTER 6

The smell of jet fuel lingered in the air as I shoved my bag into the overhead compartment. Tate and I took our seats and looked around at the other travelers. We were giddy that we harbored a secret they were not privy to. We were all on a plane to Los Angeles, but, for us, it was just a stopover to change planes. From there, we were headed to Guatemala, the starting point of a yearlong backpacking trip around the world.

Our family and friends seemed to be both envious and curious when we told them we were taking a year off to travel. This wasn't some long-held dream that we saved money for or talked about for years. We made our decision just six months before we took off, when I discovered that Starbucks was offering a new sabbatical program for partners who had been there ten years or longer. When I heard about it, I knew I wanted to be one of the first.

We had no kids and no real debt. Our only initial hesitation was out of fear of the unknown, but that wasn't enough to stop us. We knew we were capable and smart and would be able to navigate whatever came our way, both on our travels and when we got back—assuming we were coming back. We had no idea what life would be like on the other side, but we were ready for the adventure.

I announced my sabbatical when I was a business development manager in SS&M, my second promotion since joining the department. My job was to develop existing multiunit accounts and find new ones such as small hotel chains, regional corporate and university food-service providers, and restaurant chains in a four-state geography.

Starbucks was growing like crazy and had acquired Tazo Tea and Hear Music, moves intended to enhance the brand and expand the business portfolio.

The company store count was twenty-five hundred, huge growth from when I started ten years prior at the thirty-seventh store in the company. The Asia business was expanding rapidly with stores opened in China, Kuwait, Lebanon, and South Korea, in addition to the original market of Japan.

Trading the security of a good job and a relatively cushy life for a year of backpacking perplexed some people.

Tate and I were in the groove of our careers, and his construction business was going well. We were settled into our new home with our dog, Bailey, and spending all available free time in the garden.

Around us, we watched friends setting their sights on that next-level promotion or starting families. Pretty much everyone seemed to be on a path of stability and comfort. And we were choosing a completely opposite path.

But for us, there was no time like the present. Waiting would just mean that we would have other obligations like a bigger mortgage, kids, or maybe even physical health issues that would make it a challenge to travel.

The itch to do something disruptive in our lives first showed up about a year prior to our departure.

Tate and I started talking with some friends about the idea of cashing in our Starbucks stock options and opening a small inn in La Paz, Mexico, on the Baja Peninsula.

Our friends lived in Seattle but were from Mexico and looking to move back to La Paz soon. The idea appealed to us because it seemed less risky to have business partners familiar with operating in Mexico than doing it on our own. They knew the language and the business climate and had plenty of the connections we needed to get set up.

On a real estate finding trip, we visited a range of hotel and inn properties for sale, but none totally hit the mark. However, it gave us a good sense of what we wanted and what we didn't want. When we returned to Seattle, a vision of our life south of the border was becoming clearer.

Not long after we got back from that trip, our friends got pregnant and decided the timing was no longer right for them. They wanted to stay in Seattle for a while to raise their family, so we put the hotel-in-Mexico idea on the back burner but were now committed to the idea of doing *something*.

We both felt restless and bored with the status quo, although we weren't sure exactly what we wanted to do.

We bought books on community-supported agriculture and combed real estate listings for small farms. Then we had an idea to buy an inn or bed-and-breakfast closer to home, but we couldn't decide on where, and it didn't feel like the same adventure as our grand Mexico plan.

The pull of being in a completely new environment continued to tug at us, and we started to read blogs written by expats and travelers. We were inspired and energized by their stories about extensive tours of the world or courageous moves that resulted in rooting themselves somewhere far from home.

What had been the spark of an idea to do a little traveling grew into a roaring flame of desire to see the world.

One day, I came home from work to find Tate stretched out on the living room floor, hovering over a big map. He had gone to a local travel bookstore on a whim and had spent the afternoon studying places he'd always wanted to visit. I could feel the energy and excitement emanating from his body.

I had barely taken off my coat and put down my briefcase when he made a bold proposition. I could tell from the big grin on his face that his wheels must have been turning on it all day.

"We could travel eastbound and focus primarily on developing countries to save money," he said, barely looking up from the map as he traced his finger on a route that started in South America and eventually made its way over to Asia after a stop in Africa.

Butterflies immediately formed in my stomach—the idea both scared and thrilled me. Tate had been to Guatemala a few times, and my grandma took me to Israel and Europe when I was in high school, but that was pretty much the extent of our international travel experience.

It sounded exciting, but questions of doubt kept popping up in my brain. What if something happened to us physically while we were gone? What would we do with our house and our dog? What about our jobs? How much would this cost, and what if we spent it all and didn't have anything when we got back? I was the more pragmatic one in our marriage, always defaulting to carefully crafted plans that weighed the pros and cons in a logical manner.

Tate's mind moved fast and his heart even faster. He approached things he was excited about with full-on passion and optimism. Once he latched onto something, there was no going back. He wasn't pushy like a bulldog, but more enthusiastic like a lab. He knew the way to bring me along was giving me time to process and backing up an idea with an appropriate level of research and analysis.

He explained that if we kept our route to less-traveled places like Latin America and Asia, it would be a lot more affordable. Plus, Europe, the US, and Australia could wait until we were older and desired more infrastructure and creature comforts. He did some quick math to figure out how much we would need to travel and pay for any home-related expenses while we were gone. Surprisingly, it wasn't that much.

Luckily, we bought our house at a low point in the market, so we could get almost enough in rent each month to cover our mortgage. We estimated that we'd need to save about $40,000 to comfortably cover everything for up to a year, and if I socked away my bonus checks from my sales job into a savings account and watched our spending over the next six months, we would be in good shape.

With our financial plan laid out, we needed to decide what to do with our dog, Bailey, and our cat, Schmitty. Tate's sister, Shauna, graciously agreed to take the dog in, and my grandma offered to have our cat at her house in Alaska.

Everything was coming together, and we knocked down the barriers one by one. The house would be rented. We had a plan to temporarily rehome our pets. We had a savings plan and some semblance of a job-and-benefits security blanket through Starbucks's sabbatical program.

Our departure date was set for October, and the only thing left was to choose our route.

Our initial plan had us starting in Guatemala to see Tate's friends who lived there. We wouldn't be jumping into our adventure completely cold as there would be some familiarity to ease us into our travels. From there, we'd go to South America, then over to South Africa, on to East Africa, up to Egypt, over to Southeast Asia, and finally to Indonesia before returning to the States. We identified major sights we wanted to see and activities we wanted to do along the way, but we refrained from getting superdetailed with our plans so we could be fluid with our itinerary.

Our one-way air tickets took us from continent to continent, but everything in between would be figured out while we were on the road. Bucket-list items included seeing the ancient Guatemalan temples of Tikal, hiking Machu Picchu, visiting the Bolivian salt flats, exploring Torres del Paine National Park in southern Chile, going on a safari in Africa, seeing the pyramids of Egypt, and spending time in the hill country of Thailand.

Our expectations were few and our anticipation was high—the white space in our itinerary was greater than the must-see list. And the white space is where the adventure lives.

I was among the first partners to take advantage of Starbucks's brand-new sabbatical program. It was considered revolutionary at the time because sabbaticals were traditionally found in higher education, not in retail or restaurant companies. It was unpaid, but the program included a guaranteed job if I came back within one year, and my benefits remained intact while I was gone. Plus, how I spent my time off was totally at my discretion—the program was designed for long-term partners to recharge and refresh, not work.

Even though I was thirty years old and still getting established in my career, I wasn't concerned that taking time off would hurt my future because I still had plenty of years ahead of me. Not to mention that personal growth would undoubtedly come from the experience.

October arrived quickly, and there we were, waiting for the airplane door to close. Tate and I looked at one another and reached for each other's hand, excited and nervous for the year ahead. There was no turning back.

After the familiarity of visiting friends in Guatemala, the training wheels were ripped off when we got to Quito, Ecuador, our first stop in South America. We hadn't been there more than twenty-four hours when we got robbed because of a rookie-traveler move. Tate had some cash and credit cards zipped in the leg of his travel pants, and, before we knew it, he was subtly boxed in by a group of pickpockets. One of them sliced his pocket with a razor and slipped out his wallet before the group disbursed.

Fortunately, he wasn't hurt, but the boldness and invasiveness of it were startling. It was a valuable lesson, and on the rest of our travels, we exercised much more caution, especially in areas where crime was prevalent.

Unnerved by the robbery, we decided to get out of the big city the next day and took a bus to Cuenca, Ecuador, where we intended to spend a month studying Spanish. We wanted to get a solid language foundation to prepare us for the next three to four months of travel on the continent.

Cuenca is a beautiful city and a UNESCO World Heritage Site, set high in the Andes mountain range. Surrounded by lush farmland, the city of half a million is a hub for artisan crafts such as wool sweaters, Panama hats, and metal works. The colonial buildings edge up against the pristine cobblestone streets, giving the town an up-country, genteel feeling.

We were excited to call it our home for the next month, but our time in Cuenca was cut short when, after only two weeks there, we sensed unrest brewing in the city.

One evening, we were walking to our hostel from class and noticed people marching in the streets, carrying banners and shouting Spanish phrases that we didn't understand.

Every few blocks, we passed piles of burning tires on the side of the street, forcing us to cover our faces with our shirts to keep the toxic air from seeping into our lungs. We asked a local what was going on, and he told us that they were protesting the rapid devaluation of the national currency and questionable ethics by the government.

The transportation systems and staffing at government agencies were highly vulnerable. As tension mounted, we didn't want to risk our own safety or possibly get stuck in Cuenca without a way out, so we decided to leave the next day instead of continuing our lessons.

Our first stop the next morning was the ATM to get cash for bus tickets out of town. Credit cards weren't accepted many places because business owners didn't trust the banks. Things were getting so bad that they feared they might not be able to collect charges owed to them from financial institutions.

We put our debit card in the machine and pressed the withdrawal button, opting for thirty dollars, the maximum it would give us at one time, which was barely enough for two bus tickets to Peru.

The machine spit out a wad of bills almost an inch thick, and if you didn't know the exchange rate, you'd think we were clutching at least a thousand dollars in our hands. In contrast, just days earlier when we had withdrawn the same amount, the stack of bills was half the size, a physical expression of the rapid devaluation of the currency. We awkwardly stuffed the cash deep into our pockets and walked briskly back to our hostel, peeking over our shoulders on occasion to ensure we weren't about to be the target of another potential petty theft.

The bus station was chaotic when we arrived later that morning. Everyone had the same idea we did—get out before things turned for the worse. After wandering around the station, we found a bus headed for Peru that had room for us and departed that afternoon. We still had a few hours to kill but weren't about to lose our seats to someone else, so we sat on our backpacks, watching the throngs of people jostling about and the bus-ticket sellers trying to sway patient, stressed-out travelers to choose their line.

Finally, 4:00 p.m. rolled around, and we boarded our well-worn, formerly luxurious bus and settled into our seats for the thirteen-hour ride to the border. As we passed through banana plantations and lush farmland, we waved goodbye to Ecuador. It was an adventurous start to our trip around the world.

I was out of my comfort zone but kept reminding myself that this was why we took this trip—to be in a completely new environment without the creature comforts and familiarity of home.

Right after the sun came up, a small Ecuadorian town appeared on the horizon, signaling that we were entering civilization after our overnight trip through jungle and desolate deserts.

The bus slowed, and the driver ordered us off. We didn't see any buildings or signs that we were at the border and at first had no idea where we were or what was going on.

Taking in our surroundings, we could see the town we stopped in was a total dump. The river flowing through the center was brown and filled with garbage. Ramshackle huts and dilapidated structures cobbled together from scrap material dotted the riverbanks, making for unsanitary living conditions. There was no notable architecture, and the only businesses open were a few sidewalk food stands where enterprising cooks prepared *llapingachos* (potato patties with cheese) on dirty-looking grills for a breakfast on the go.

At the bus driver's insistence, we disembarked and grabbed our large backpacks from the storage underneath. He gesticulated broadly in a direction away from the town, but there was nothing ahead of us except an open road and tumbleweeds. We were totally perplexed until another tourist explained that the border was right in front of us, but passport control and customs were up the road a few kilometers. Although this was our first ever overland border crossing, it seemed very strange and a little scary.

We exchanged some dollars for Peruvian soles even though we had no idea what the exchange rate was (after all, this was the late nineties; it wasn't like we could just pull our iPhones out) and proceeded to walk in the direction the driver pointed.

After a couple of minutes, we noticed we were being followed by a neatly dressed, clean-cut man carrying a newspaper tucked under his arm. We were suspicious and grabbed our packs more tightly in case of a potential robbery. This was a hard-worn town, and I'm sure we looked like rich, vulnerable tourists with our ExOfficio clothes and the camera bag dangling from Tate's neck. Our Quito experience taught us to be more judicious, so we had hidden money all over our bodies, including underneath the inserts in our shoes just in case.

Noticing our border-crossing conundrum, the man with the newspaper approached us and offered to drive us to the passport station in his Dodge Charger for a small fee. We were wary. Even though his car looked clean and seemed to be running well, the horror stories of other travelers made us question whether this was a good idea. We'd heard of unsuspecting tourists in some of these more remote and/or sketchy towns where crime was high, trusting an earnest-appearing local looking to make a few dollars as a private "taxi," only to be driven out to a remote area, robbed, and left stranded with no way back. This was a future we certainly didn't want for ourselves. But we were in the middle of nowhere and we couldn't see any other options, so we decided to go for it.

The driver offered to put our bags in his trunk, but we weren't taking any chances and insisted that we have them up front on our laps. We reluctantly climbed into the back seat of his car and pulled the creaking doors closed after verifying that there were working internal door handles so we could escape if we needed to (a safety measure we read about in travel blogs). We were beyond paranoid but didn't know how else we were going to get to the Peruvian immigration building kilometers down the road. As the car started, Tate and I looked at each other, held hands tightly, and said a silent wish that we would come out on the other side.

To our surprise and gratitude, five minutes later, we arrived at the immigration building and exhaled a sigh of relief. We had miraculously avoided being one of those horror stories we read about.

We thanked our driver, hopped out of his car, and walked the few yards to the immigration office to get our passports stamped and cross into Peru. We'd made it. It was my first real act of bravery and courage on our trip and one that is forever indelible in my mind.

Growth comes from discomfort, and that experience pushed me to the edge.

* * *

Two months later, we decided to take a "break" from our travels to spend the holidays in Chile with some other travelers we met. We found a large beachfront condo with enough beds to sleep all seven of us and were thrilled to be back in civilization for a week.

There were huge American-style grocery stores stocked with everything imaginable. The shopping malls were decked out for the holidays with Christmas music playing, and the city parks were beyond gorgeous with lush palm trees and tropical flowers.

We were like kids in a candy store and reveled in the ability to cook our own meals after two months of eating in restaurants. We decorated our condo walls with Christmas wrapping paper and ribbon and bought candles to add holiday ambience.

But despite the pretty white sand beaches and all the amenities we desired at our fingertips, I found it difficult to fully enjoy our newfound bounty.

I was emotionally overwhelmed by the extreme homeless-animal population.

Everywhere we went, there were disarmingly mangy dogs, often hairless due to skin infections. Cats were just as bad, with many missing limbs, eyes, or ears, fighting over scraps on the dock where the fishermen cast the waste from their morning's catch.

While my travel companions frolicked in the waves, I couldn't shake the images of the neglected street animals out of my head. They fought for survival every moment of every day, and I wanted to save them all.

I wrote furiously about my feelings in my travel journal, scrawling about the need for a national spay-and-neuter program. I envisioned creating a network of shelters to provide proper veterinary care for the poor creatures. The task seemed daunting, not just because of the volume of need but because it was a huge cultural undertaking. These animals ended up on the streets because of lack of knowledge and lack of resources, but I still felt compelled to do something to help them.

I pleaded with Tate to stop our travels and stay in Chile. I suggested we use our remaining trip savings to live there and fund animal welfare projects. Yes, it seemed like a herculean task, but if we didn't do it, who would? I cried for three days straight, and, on our last night there, Tate told me that if I still felt this way by the time we got to Argentina, we could come back and take on my mission. I was grateful for his empathetic yet rational heart—he may have thought I was crazy, but he never let on.

Pictures of the homeless cats and dogs were seared into my mind, but, as our travels continued, I realized that my grand ambitions were a bit unrealistic. Trying to change a whole culture and societal system required more money and energy than I had to give. I decided I would channel my love for animals when I got back to the States—there was plenty of need closer to home, and I became a regular volunteer at animal shelters when we returned.

We said goodbye to South America after four months of traveling down the Andes and welcomed the exploration of a new continent, Africa.

Our primary objective for our stop in Africa was to go on safari. We did a self-drive safari in South Africa and a walking safari in Zimbabwe before we made our way to Tanzania.

The day before we were to head out to explore the great plains of the Serengeti and Ngorongoro Crater, I was in an internet café in the small city of Arusha.

The ceiling fans whirred overhead, and the sterile decor with white tile and rows of computer stations clearly conveyed the purpose of the café—functional. This was a place people came to get news, communicate with friends and family, or to take care of school or business matters.

Amid the junk mail, I saw an email from my grandma with the subject line "Your Grandpa." I knew it wasn't going to be good news—he had been battling colon cancer for a couple of years.

My grandpa's quiet demeanor made him hard to get to know in a deeply personal way, but I held him in the highest regard for his calm wisdom, a style that was in direct contrast to the domineering personalities of many of my other family members. He was never brash or judgmental and was always full of curiosity about the world and people.

My grandma's note confirmed my fears—my grandfather had passed peacefully in his sleep a few days prior, and his memorial was scheduled in four weeks.

We couldn't have been farther away from Fairbanks, Alaska, but, after much deliberation, we decided to head back to the US for his funeral and changed our itinerary to skip Egypt and resume our travels afterward in Nepal.

I was overwhelmed by the turnout for my grandfather's funeral, which was held in a theater on the grounds of a city park. The state lieutenant governor spoke about the impact he had on Alaska, and when the military color guard presented the flag to my grandmother and then played "Taps," tears streamed down my face.

We spent a week visiting with family and then boarded a plane, yet again, this time headed for Nepal.

On our first morning in Kathmandu, we awoke to the cacophony of a waking city—bleating horns, crowing roosters, loudspeakers blaring advertisements, and the roar of various motorized contraptions without mufflers.

The streets teemed with people on their way to work and school artfully dodging the tuk tuks, cars, and cattle going every which way. There didn't seem to be any rules of the road as far as we could tell, except that whoever was boldest usually had the right of way. Occasionally, there would be a seemingly random spot of red powder on the road or sidewalk, a demarcation of a holy or spiritual occurrence as part of Hindu tradition.

Smells of burning incense, cooking oil, and gasoline filled the air, and, although we weren't wearing them, masks would have been a good idea, given all the pollution. Vendors pushed carts filled with snacks, building supplies, and household goods down narrow alleys framed by poorly built stick-and-brick buildings that looked like they'd crumble if you leaned against them too hard.

We decided to do an eight-day trek from Jomsom to Muktinath and hired an enterprising young man named Hiran whom we'd read about in a travel blog. I had never done a multiday hike before and was both nervous and excited. Trekking in Nepal was going to be as much a physical experience as it was a cultural one. We'd be visiting remote villages and staying with local families.

Getting to the start of the trek was an adventure in and of itself. A death-defying and harrowing bus ride from Kathmandu to Pokhara elevated our heart rates as the driver careened around the corners of the mountain highway, steep cliffs dropping below us. The wheels of the bus screeched as they rubbed inside the wheel wells on the especially sharp corners. One slight wrong move and we'd all be dead.

From Pokhara, we boarded a small plane for the twenty-minute flight to Jomsom, the starting point of our trek, at an elevation of almost ten thousand feet.

Our plane leveled out briefly before its descent, and the sheer mountain faces outside our windows looked close enough to touch. Soaring high above our small plane, they jutted up into the sky, reminding us of the magnitude of the Himalayas. We were but a tiny speck among them. It was nothing short of astounding.

As soon as we landed, we hopped out of the plane, got our trekking permits, and immediately started our journey. Each day, we'd hike six to eight hours, up and down mountain passes and through extreme landscapes.

Our guesthouse accommodations were very primitive, but they gave us a glimpse as to how people in such remote locations lived. One village where we stayed was known for its apples, and we were rewarded at the end of a long day with apple brandy and apple pie. Another village was full of families practicing polyandry, whereby the woman of the house takes two or more husbands, a customary way to keep wealth in the family. The village of Muktinath at the base of the Annapurna massif attracted pilgrims from all over the world. They descended on the different shrines, keeping their prayer wheels in constant motion, the smell of melted ghee candles filling the air.

Taking in all the sights and learning about the cultures, customs, and uniqueness of each microregion kept our long days engaging. Hiran was a wonderful guide. He was knowledgeable about the area and sensed when to allow silence and reflection that came with the spiritual nature of a journey like ours. There was a lot to take in and absorb.

Midway through our trek, my body started feeling the cumulative effects of fatigue and the altitude. Not only had we started our trek at well over nine thousand feet; we had climbed over four thousand feet since we left Jomsom five days previously, and, while our route wasn't very technical, there had been a lot of elevation gain and drop each day.

Hiran told us that our destination for the night was just a couple more hours away, and we needed to go over the next pass via a stone staircase to get there. I could see the steep stairs climbing through the lush green forest, with no end in sight. Normally, I would have marveled at the work it took to build this part of the trail, but instead, I became overwhelmed by what was ahead. My legs suddenly felt like they weighed one hundred pounds each, and I didn't think I could take another step. I took off my pack and sat down at the bottom of the staircase, put my head in my hands, and started weeping. Every bone in my body was tired, and I wanted to stop right there. My mind swirled with negative thoughts of not finishing as I saw other trekkers pass by out of the corner of my eye.

Tate and Hiran offered plenty of encouragement as I worked to pull myself together and find strength within. I knew there was only one way to get down the mountain, and it would have to be on my own two legs. Mule transport was for the sick and injured, not for the healthy but tired backpacker.

When I decided I was ready to give it a try, Hiran graciously carried my pack for me in addition to his own, because he could see how much I was struggling.

Instead of focusing on the fact that we had three more days left of our trek, I decided to focus on just ten stairs at a time. This made the ascent more manageable and less overwhelming, both physically and emotionally. Climb ten stairs, then rest. Climb ten more stairs, and I could have a snack. Climb another ten stairs, and I would get to admire the view behind me. Climb another ten stairs, and I'd be that much closer to dinner. And so it went, until we finally reached the top.

When we arrived in the village on the other side of the pass, I collapsed with exhaustion but was also filled with pride. I had just accomplished something that I didn't think I had in me. I didn't grow up doing outdoorsy things, had never been much of a hiker, and the word "athletic" was never used to describe me.

But here I was, about to complete an eight-day trek through Nepal.

I could do hard things. Bravery and fortitude kept me going.

* * *

Our sabbatical was full of experiences that stretched me physically and emotionally. Each day presented some sort of challenge or learning moment, intensified by language barriers, infrastructure gaps, and cultural differences.

My confidence as well as my problem-solving and perseverance skills were honed through daily practice. The sabbatical felt like I was on a fast-tracked personal development plan but with a much higher level of exposure and vulnerability. It was so much more than an extended vacation—it was transformative. And I couldn't wait to live my life differently when I got back.

It was a bit of a culture shock touching down in Seattle after 365 days on the road. Everything looked so shiny and bright, I almost had to squint to see. White light seemed to emanate from the glass high-rise buildings towering over the city, and late-model cars whizzed by me on the highway.

After a year of staying in primitive lodging and riding in vehicles older than I was on dusty, pothole-ridden roads, our city suddenly looked embarrassingly prosperous.

This first glimpse of reentry into a "normal" life after our sabbatical set the tone for finding our way back into our family, work, and society. I was a mix of excited and a little disoriented. I experienced so much in the last year, but I wasn't sure how to process it, much less share it.

My gratitude for the basics taken for granted in the US such as clean water and healthy food was even more profound. My life priorities and values had crystalized. I didn't want to work like a dog and be disengaged from things that mattered most to me. I wanted to be more present and carve out time for things that brought me growth and enrichment.

I struggled with how to express the life-changing moments I had on our travels. They were begging to come out, but how could others truly understand what I went through? How could I convey the emotion I felt when I crossed that mountain pass in Nepal and the exhausted exhilaration and sense of accomplishment when I got to the other side? I didn't know how to articulate what I went through so that it was relevant, and I struggled with what to do with the bouncing energy that it created.

Feeling renewed, refreshed, and ready to tackle the next challenge, I walked back into the Starbucks Support Center. I felt different, but I couldn't describe how. I was excited to be back at work, but part of me yearned for life on the road and how each day brought a completely new and unchartered experience.

The welcome-back wagon was filled with curious coworkers wanting to know where I went and what my favorite place was. That was an impossible question to answer. Each town, city, and country was so different from all the others, there was no single favorite spot. Beyond the usual sightseeing and tourist experiences, the people we met and our physical, mental, and emotional journey were what imprinted the most profound memories.

It didn't take me long to realize that my experience was uniquely mine. None of my colleagues had taken a year off from work to travel the world with their life partner like I did. No matter how hard I tried to convey what I experienced, I felt oddly out of sync and unable to relate to them. It felt like my pace of change and growth on the road was accelerated, and my perception was that it moved more slowly for everyone else while I was gone.

Transitioning back in was harder than I expected. I felt very untethered those first few months. I had no official job or job title—in the HR system, I was called "professional unclassified." My old job was restructured, leaving me without a formal role for a full year after I returned. Even though I was brimming with pent-up enthusiasm that came with the renewal from my time away, I felt lost.

Frustrations aside, I made the most of the opportunity to contribute and grow my career, and I jumped in where I felt I could add value. I treated it like my travels by deciding to go with the flow and see how it all played out. Instead of letting the uncertainty fill me with anxiety, I embraced it and considered it an opportunity to be creative and learn new things.

Tom, my mentor who helped me get into Specialty Sales and Marketing in the first place, had been promoted to vice president by the time I returned and had remained my steadfast advocate while I was out.

He did a great job of keeping me front and center with Gregg, the new senior vice president of our business unit, while I was gone. He kept an eye and ear toward where I might land when I got back and recommended that I support one of Gregg's top priorities. Gregg was looking to put in a new customer relationship management software system and needed help understanding the department workflow. He knew that a new system couldn't be designed around broken processes and asked for my help to figure it out.

Even without an official job title or team, I was excited about the project because the work was new to me and would provide me breadth and perspective across the whole department. It was something I could sink my teeth into even though I knew nothing about implementing IT systems. But I did know how to do research and wasn't shy about picking up the phone and asking questions to uncover how things worked or didn't.

The project gave me unique access to the senior leaders of the department, including exposure to Gregg and his team. He had been the head of Starbucks US retail business prior to leading our group and had a solid reputation for being a great people leader and good businessperson.

I can still picture Gregg's genuine smile and care when he talked with others. His whole face lit up, eyes twinkling behind his smallish glasses. He'd lean in with his tall, lithe frame capped by a head of curly hair, earnestly listening to what people had to say. On Fridays, he went into full-on casual mode, wearing baggy old blue jeans and Birkenstocks with socks, making him not only approachable but relatable—at least to the hippies on our team.

Supersmart and curious, he was less "corporate" than other executives I had been exposed to, and he didn't take himself too seriously. Gregg created an atmosphere of both performance and fun, and the rest of us were encouraged to participate.

After a couple of months of research and documenting my findings on the current organizational processes, I discovered inefficiencies in how the team members worked with each other and with customers, confirming Gregg's intuition. Implementing a new customer-relationship management system wouldn't solve the problem. To work optimally, the department would need to be restructured. The bottom line was that the project needed to shift focus from system design and implementation to organizational design.

After I shared my recommendation with Gregg, he asked me to come to one of his leadership meetings to present my findings and ask for the group's support to undertake a deeper organizational assessment.

I knew going into the meeting and glossing over the situation wouldn't be helpful to the business, partners, or customers. Even if what I was going to recommend might be controversial, it was what they needed to hear.

Nerves rumbled inside me when I walked into the room even though the leadership team seemed in good spirits. Gregg's direct-report team was an affable group of very down-to-earth executives, and I was generally able to be myself when I was with them, but this meeting felt like a big deal. They were expecting a project update, not a recommendation to change the organizational structure they had implemented right after I went on sabbatical.

I went to the head of the table, said hello to everyone, and plugged in my laptop to fire up my PowerPoint presentation.

And then I got straight to the point—to really solve the problems at hand, a department reorganization was needed.

As I spoke, I looked around the table and was surprised to notice people nodding in agreement. They were in full alignment—they had been feeling the pain points themselves.

I breathed a sigh of relief. Thank goodness I wasn't way off base. If I was, who knew where it would lead for me and my career.

Fortunately, as an outcome of my recommendation, Gregg asked me to lead the organizational design effort with a colleague in the Learning and Development department, and we had a new structure two months later.

It also meant that, a full year after I returned from sabbatical, I finally had a permanent job. I was now a regional sales manager, and, for the first time in my career, I had a team of people to lead.

I may have eventually gotten this role without a sabbatical, but the unique opportunity to do a temporary assignment working for a Starbucks senior executive was never something I had considered before I left for my trip. Projects like these were few and far between and usually reserved for partners identified as high potential and at the director level and above. There were a ton of unexpected benefits, including giving me unique exposure and practical experience in communicating with senior business leaders.

My travels around the world undoubtedly prepared me for a year of working in ambiguity and building my confidence. While I felt lost and not understood when I first returned, I could now see the direct benefit of my time off, even if it wasn't overt to others.

I had grown through the discomfort of my travels and the discomfort of my reentry, and it paid off with a meaty new job and expanded responsibilities.

Finding comfort amid the discomfort continued to be a theme in my life.

CHAPTER 7

"You are twelve going on thirty," my aunt Perri used to tell me.

I swelled with pride at what I thought was the ultimate compliment. It had nothing to do with my looks but was all about my fierce desire to be a grown-up and have independence.

I took my role in our family as the oldest child and oldest cousin very seriously. Because I didn't have a lot of parental engagement or oversight, I was forced to take care of myself at a young age. Whether it was cooking a meal for my brother and me, taking the city bus to get around, or muddling my way through my difficult math homework solo, I pretty much had to figure out most things on my own. I wasn't neglected; it was just that my dad had limited resources and capacity, and my mom wasn't around.

Without a lot of childcare options, my brother, Jason, and I were often left to our own devices—good and bad. One time when our dad went out of town for the weekend, Jason and I decided to have a party at our house. After all, that was what middle schoolers did in Fairbanks, Alaska.

Word traveled fast for a time when there weren't cell phones, and over fifty people showed up. I didn't know half of them, a mix of classmates and, oddly, adults I'd never seen before. I had no idea why they would want to party with a bunch of underage kids.

Jason and I scurried around, trying to contain the pot smoking and make sure nothing got broken. As I unclogged a toilet that had been stuffed with a whole roll of toilet paper, the cops rolled up and told everyone to go home before someone got hurt or arrested. Miraculously, our dad never found out, or, if he did, he didn't let on.

As I moved through high school, I had a few other shenanigans like the eighth-grade party, but, once I entered my senior year, I had a one-track mind to graduate and get out of Fairbanks. I wanted to make a life where I could support myself without relying on others.

I saw myself as a strong career woman, fully in charge of my own destiny and not overly reliant on others. I wasn't looking to settle down. Marriage, much less starting a family, was never in my life vision.

And then I met Tate.

We started dating when I was twenty-three, and we were married three years later. Even though marriage wasn't part of my grand plan, we enjoyed each other's company, and Tate's gentility and kindness taught me that I didn't want to be alone.

Five years after we wed, starting a family was still absent from our vision. We enjoyed the freedom and flexibility of having two incomes and no kids and just couldn't picture the restrictions that would come with having someone else to be responsible for. Having a dog tied us down enough as it was.

But our sabbatical trip around the world changed all that.

We saw how important the family structure was in different cultures and knew that we could create our own way of living as a family unit. Having kids didn't mean we needed to pump the brakes on our dreams and hobbies; we might just need to think about them a little bit differently. We'd always envisioned becoming old together but could now imagine how quiet life might be if it were just the two of us and, even worse, when one of us passed and left the other one completely alone.

Eighteen months after we returned from our travels, I decided to see my primary care doctor to make sure I was a healthy thirty-two-year-old and ready to take on the physical endeavor of pregnancy. When I asked her what I should expect in terms of how long it might take to conceive, she told me about eighteen months, given my age and family history. If it all worked out and we didn't have any problems, we might have a baby by the time I was thirty-five. Even so, I knew that pregnancy wasn't guaranteed, and there was always the possibility of complications or problems conceiving.

Tate and I sat with this information for a few months, still mulling over whether we wanted to take on such a huge commitment. This was a decision for life and not one to be taken lightly, especially since we weren't that couple that always knew we wanted to have kids. We decided to try seeing what would happen and let fate take its course. If we got pregnant, great. If we didn't, it wasn't meant to be.

We celebrated our momentous decision with a long-anticipated trip to Greece. We had dreamed of the white-washed buildings, deep blue sea, and authentic Greek food for years.

After a few days in Athens, we settled on the island of Santorini for a couple of nights and kept extending our stay, eventually canceling our plans to visit the other islands. We were perfectly content taking in the sparkling crystal waters and jaw-dropping sunsets from our suite perched on the edge of the caldera. Lazy walks on the meandering stone pathways were an effortless way to soak up the peacefulness of the small town of Oia. We had everything we needed.

When we got back to Seattle, sun-kissed and relaxed, I took my first home pregnancy test, fully expecting it to be negative. I'd been off the pill a few months to cleanse my body, and

Greece was the first time ever that we hadn't used any sort of birth control. According to my doctor, we were at the beginning of a long road to conception.

When I glanced down at the test, I did a double take and rubbed my eyes. The test clearly displayed a line indicating it was positive. We were going to be parents.

I was shaking in disbelief, a combination of both elation and pure panic. I waited impatiently for Tate to get home from work so I could tell him, and when he finally walked in the front door, I pounced on him with nervous excitement.

"I'm pregnant!" I practically shouted.

His mouth fell open in disbelief. "Are you sure?"

We were both in a bit of shock. I showed him the pregnancy-test stick, and we squinted hard to make sure we weren't seeing things. Yep, there was definitely a line in the window of the test stick—we were pregnant. A follow-up appointment with my doctor confirmed it a few weeks later. There was no going back now.

Fortunately, I was healthy and strong during my pregnancy and didn't need to slow down at work or in any other aspect of my life. I charged hard as usual.

My scope in Business Alliances had grown from the interim special projects role when I returned from sabbatical, to managing a territory that included everything west of the Mississippi. I had team members in five different states and loved what I was doing, even if it meant traveling almost every week.

With the baby and my belly growing, I bought a tiny suitcase that held a black maternity power suit and a few toiletries, everything I needed for an overnight trip.

I maintained a healthy stamina until my seventh month of pregnancy, when I started getting tired faster and found I was needing more sleep. Although it wasn't shocking, it was frustrating. My mind wanted to keep going at the same pace, but my body was not having it.

I had one last business trip in early December and was looking forward to having it behind me. Most of my customers were on the West Coast, but one of my top prospects, a national hotel chain, asked me to come to New York to see their new flagship property.

We'd been in negotiations for months, and this meeting could put a bow on the deal right before I went on maternity leave. It was a long way to go for one night, but it was really important for the company, and I wanted to see it through. My boss, Matt, was also going, along with a team member who had been involved and would oversee the account while I was on maternity leave.

Matt and I worked together less than a year, and, for some reason, I often felt a step behind him. He came off as savvy and was a smooth talker, his depth of business development experience far exceeding mine. One-on-ones with him were often instructional, where he would grab a pen and paper and sketch a diagram or hash out a business math problem to make a teaching point.

Matt and Tom, my long-time mentor, were peer vice presidents, but their personalities contrasted starkly. Tom was competitive but genuinely loved his team and was sometimes overly emotional. Matt was equally competitive, but his intensity seemed to be driven by a winning-at-all-costs mindset.

With Starbucks's touchy-feely relationship-oriented culture, Matt tried to soften his image with doses of levity. There was always a feeling that you couldn't quite completely relax around him even though he was often calm and seemed unflappable. The only tell that something ruffled him was a close-mouthed half smile accompanied by raised eyebrows. When he was upset, it could have been skepticism, disappointment, or anger underneath, but you never really knew. I think the fact that he had been in the US Marines deeply imprinted a composed and command-and-control leadership style.

Matt carried himself with assurance, aided by his lean six-feet-two frame. He was a good-looking man with piercing blue eyes, perfectly straight teeth, and thick, wavy, light-brown hair. With his chiseled jaw, he could have easily been mistaken for a movie star.

His clothes were always perfectly pressed, and he kept his office neat and orderly. Even though he had four young sons at home and traveled frequently for his job, he managed to find time to work out regularly and was very fit. At a department meeting once, Tom referred to himself as a twin for hippie comedian Cheech from the *Cheech and Chong* movies in contrast to Matt, who he claimed was more like Jack LaLanne, the ageless founding father of fitness and health.

In preparation for our flight to New York, Matt and I had agreed to sit next to each other on the plane so we could do some final preparations for our sales call. He mentioned that he also wanted to talk with me about a few things related to my upcoming leave. As much as I wanted to sleep on the plane, I knew this wasn't going to be an option.

After the beverage cart rolled through, I turned my body to an angle that enabled me to reach around my belly and grab my notepad and pen from underneath the seat in front of me. Even the smallest tasks were getting hard to do. I was well into my third trimester and starting to experience the physical limitations that came with a baby growing inside me.

I started taking notes for our meeting, but Matt opened the conversation on a different topic.

"So, Christine. What are your plans for when you return from maternity leave?"

His question caused me to pause. I had always intended to keep doing what I was doing—managing national accounts for the Western division.

"I plan on coming back to this job, of course," I said, hoping I sounded more confident than I felt. "I haven't considered doing anything different and don't want to."

In reality, I was a little nervous about how I was going to handle a new baby with weekly travel, long hours, and the stress of a large financial target. But I'd cross that bridge when I came to it—for the time being, I was committed to the job.

While I spoke, Matt looked down at his tray table and shook his head.

"You know, Christine," he said, "I'm not sure if this is the right role for you, or if sales is the right place. We'll see what happens when you get back from leave, but right now, I just don't see it. Some people are made for sales, and others are not."

He turned to the notepad in front of him, took a sip of his water, and continued.

"How about when we go into this sales call tomorrow, I'll take the lead. Who knows if you're going to come back anyway? John and I got this. You don't need to worry about this account anymore."

I sat there stunned. Here I was seven months pregnant, flying across the country to close a deal I had been working on for months, and my boss told me he didn't have confidence in me and was going to take over. I wanted nothing more than to ask the pilots to turn the plane around and go back to Seattle.

Instead, I clamped my mouth shut, looked away, and tried hard not to cry. My hormones were all out of whack; I was exhausted; and Matt's comments weren't just poorly timed— they were mind-blowingly inappropriate.

I shut my notebook and took a few deep breaths, trying to remain composed. No need for me to spend any more energy on preparations; my role had just been diminished to that of hostess.

As pissed off as I felt, I was too tired to put up a fight. Instead, I acquiesced.

"Um, okay," was all I said, and then closed my eyes to avoid further conversation.

After our flight landed around 10:00 p.m., I went straight to the hotel and tried to sleep. But I was so worked up from the conversation with Matt (not to mention the general discomfort of late pregnancy) that I tossed and turned for hours. I wondered if I should have said something more to him on the flight, but I honestly felt stuck—he was going to be dictating where and what I did in Business Alliances no matter what. He made it abundantly clear that he didn't have confidence in me as a sales leader.

I woke up at 2:30 a.m. Seattle time to meet Matt and John for breakfast so we could finalize our agenda for the customer meeting.

After showering and donning my maternity power suit and supportive footwear, I made my way to the hotel restaurant, bleary eyed and exhausted. I was dying for a cup of non-decaf coffee but was committed to following my doctor's orders.

Matt and John were already at a table, and I noticed that their plates were half-empty. There were no notebooks in sight, so I assumed that they hadn't yet reviewed the meeting outline. I ordered breakfast and then suggested we do one final review of our agenda as a team.

But I was too late. The two of them had hashed it out before I got there, and Matt reminded me of our discussion on the plane—I was to follow his lead.

I felt like vomiting up my omelet and hash browns, and it had nothing to do with being pregnant. The whole situation made me sick to my stomach. It wasn't fair, and it was completely disrespectful to my efforts of getting the deal so close to the finish line in the first place. I felt powerless.

My appetite gone, I suggested we head to the meeting room. The sooner we got the meeting started, the sooner it would be over and I'd be on a plane home.

Our customers were waiting in the meeting room for us, as excited to have us in New York as we were to be there with them. I exchanged greetings and hugs with them, our relationship warmed by the many conversations on the phone leading up to this meeting and a past trip of mine to their corporate headquarters in Memphis. I reminded myself that it was my ability to connect and sell that got us there in the first place.

I turned on as much energy as I could physically and emotionally rally and introduced Matt and John to the two executives for the first time.

After a brief, cordial exchange, we sat down at the conference table to begin the discussions. Matt and John deftly positioned themselves on either side of the clients, leaving me farthest away at the end of the table.

Matt immediately took the lead in the conversation just as he said he would, and the clients glanced in my direction, looking at me for confirmation. I nodded and corroborated the points that were made to give them confidence that they were in good hands, even though part of me just wanted to run out of the room. I figured smiling and nodding were better than punching Matt, which was what I really wanted to do.

The meeting was a success, and we got a commitment to move forward. My six months of hard work paid off, and I only regretted that I wasn't going to be there for the implementation, which would start right as I was going to be at home taking care of my new baby.

In the taxi back to the airport, Matt and John high-fived each other and talked excitedly about the next steps. I didn't say a word and was relieved that I was departing from a different terminal. I wanted to get as far away from the situation as possible.

Once through security, I huddled in a corner of the gate waiting area and started crying softly. The whole situation was frustrating, and I was beyond tired from the long flight the previous day and lack of sleep.

I called Tate from the airport and told him what happened. As always, he jumped immediately to my defense, which made me cry harder. I couldn't get home fast enough to fall into his arms.

I had no idea how I was going to manage a newborn baby and a demanding job, and I started to wonder if there was a grain of truth to what Matt said on the plane.

Maybe I wasn't cut out for this line of work. I questioned my ability as the self-doubt crept in. Being pregnant and hormonal seemed to exacerbate my feelings of insecurity. I wasn't sure where I fit in at work and had no idea what parenthood would bring. My identity was unraveling, and I didn't know where to turn.

I did what I do best in times of stress and uncertainty and busied myself with getting ready for my upcoming leave. For the next six weeks, I focused on wrapping up my deliverables and setting my team and business up for success during my impending absence. Even with Matt's comments on our way to New York, I acted as if I were going to come back to the same role. I wasn't going to let him make the decision for me.

* * *

My beautiful baby boy, Nicholas Tate McHugh, arrived ten days ahead of schedule, weighing in at a whopping nine pounds, one ounce. His early arrival foreshadowed my new reality. When you have kids, schedules go sideways all the time. I had to let go of my vision of leaving my job totally buttoned up—Nick had other plans in store for me.

The first few weeks of motherhood were hazy from lack of sleep and learning Nick's cues. As my body recovered and I adjusted to the daily patterns of feeding, sleeping, and diaper changing, I started venturing out on walks and car rides to get out of the house as much as possible.

Trying to find the balance of what I felt I could do physically and what I wanted to do meant constant trial and error. I got ambitious one sunny spring day and decided to take Nick for a walk in the stroller to the commercial area in my neighborhood. I was feeling housebound, and the call of the birds chirping and flowers blooming begged for me to get outside. The one-and-one-half-mile walk was joyous, and my face flushed from the much-needed exercise.

When it was time to turn around, I wasn't even halfway home, and fatigue suddenly set in. In that moment, I realized that my body was still recovering from childbirth, and I was too exhausted to keep walking. I broke down in tears, unsure how I was going to get home. Uber didn't exist; I wasn't near a bus line; and Tate was working across town. I decided to sit down and rest, and when my energy was restored, I pressed on. It wasn't unlike my trekking experience in Nepal—when I was at my most vulnerable and doubtful, I had to dig into my reserves to find strength to keep going.

A couple of months into my maternity leave, I started to feel a little stir-crazy and bored. I had heard stories from other parents and read magazines that described the early infant days as joyous and miraculous, but I wasn't feeling it. I wasn't depressed, but I desperately craved adult interaction, and pretty much everyone I knew was at work.

The few friends I had while on leave were stay-at-home moms who had routines of their own. Grateful for their support, I initiated a couple of social interactions but for some reason, felt like I didn't belong. Maybe it was because I knew I'd be going back to work and wouldn't be able to sustain the relationship with midday walks and coffees. Or maybe it was because I couldn't relate to their days filled with kid-related activities as I was craving my work responsibilities so much and had no desire to be at home full-time.

Getting anxious even though I still had a couple of months before I was expected back at work, I talked with my Partner Resources manager about job options when I returned. While I loved my job, traveling every week wasn't going to work for me or my family with a newborn.

This was what Matt may have seen coming. I started to wonder if the conversation on the plane was out of empathetic anticipation of how I would feel on my return to work, or if he truly believed I wasn't cut out for the job. I may never know, but the tug in my heart over my job and my new role as a parent created a swell of internal conflict.

Until then, work had been everything to me. Since I was a kid, I had wanted an important office job, and I finally had one.

I loved what I was doing, but the only field sales jobs that were big enough to challenge me and at my level required regular multistate travel. I could already tell that the demands of motherhood and my desire to prioritize Nick at this stage in his life were more important than my current job. This was my purpose, at least until I felt otherwise.

After agonizing, I decided to go back to the Training department, the group I left seven years prior for what was supposed to be a brief rotational assignment into SS&M. The training function was familiar to me. I wouldn't have to travel as much, and there was much less pressure than in a sales position, all pluses for a new mom. Even though it seemed like the best option at the time, I kept reminding myself that the decision didn't have to be forever but just for now.

This was the first time (but definitely not the last) I had to approach decision-making about my life and career differently than in the past. I now had a child I was responsible for, not just myself. The concept of maintaining a work/life blend was at the forefront of my mind. It wasn't about balance and keeping things equal but figuring out how to meld it all together effectively.

One day while I was still on leave, Pennington, my new manager in the Training department, called me to check in and ask how everything was going. I was in the middle of sweeping the front porch with Nick strapped to my body in a front-facing baby carrier. He was having a good day, and everyone had slept well the night before, so my report to her was positive. I felt like I was starting to get the hang of motherhood, even though I was eager to return to work.

Not even minutes after Pennington and I hung up, Nick had a total meltdown, causing me to do the same. Suddenly, I felt like I had no control. My desire to have independence was at an all-time high. I threw the broom and sat down on the porch sobbing, guilt settling in. How could I do the things that filled me up while also raising a child?

I missed my work, and I missed my colleagues. I missed talking about stuff besides poop, sleep cycles, and feeding challenges. There was constantly laundry to do, breast milk to pump, and diapers to change. I had been on maternity leave over two months. I craved intellectual stimulation. I was bouncing off the walls and needed something more.

I called Pennington back a couple of hours later, crying, and asked her if there was anything I could do remotely while on leave. She tried to soothe me and encouraged me to take advantage of my time off because I wouldn't be able to get it back again. In reality, Nick's day care at the Starbucks Support Center wasn't going to be able to take him in for at least two more months anyway, so I didn't have any other options but to wait it out and find a way to take care of my needs in the interim too. And that started with finding time for myself to take solo walks or read a book while Tate cared for Nick.

When I finally returned to work after four months off, I was enthusiastic for adult interaction and grateful to stimulate my mind. Of course, I loved Nick with all my heart and looked forward to seeing him each evening, but I had needs too.

The internal conflict and guilt were ever present. Being a parent meant that I had to have flexibility and let go a bit. The fact of the matter was that my time, energy, and money were going to be at the mercy of another human being, at least for the next two decades if not the rest of my life.

Motherhood is full of conundrums. Finding balance between giving to our families and trying to find space for ourselves is a constant quest. Once I became a mom, the struggle of finding my identity and balancing my career never fully went away, even with my son gearing up to go to college.

Deep down, I know that the fulfillment I get from work and my hobbies keeps me grounded and whole, and, while I've never felt completely free of guilt, I eventually found a rhythm that worked for me. I made time to go to the gym, to see friends, and to let Nick play by himself without me hovering over him twenty-four seven.

What started out as mixed feelings about going back into the Training department when I returned from maternity leave ended up being a decision I was happy about. It provided more family balance and the opportunity to work on broad, strategic projects.

It was a blend I could live with. In the end, it took me doing my best not to try to be all things to all people but to be all things to myself.

CHAPTER 8

"Who created these? They look antiseptic. They look like they've been outsourced." Howard Schultz pointed at the training materials on the conference room table.

I was the most junior person in a room full of the top executives in the company, and current circumstances necessitated this meeting to save the company.

I spoke first and without hesitation.

"My team did, and, yes, they were outsourced. We wanted to improve the visual design and learning effectiveness of the materials. The content was written by my team and provided to the vendor."

There was no reason for me to hide or deflect his comment to someone else, even if the decision to outsource the materials was made before I stepped into the role. Store barista training was now my responsibility. I needed to own this instead of someone else bumbling their way through it, trying to cover for me.

After a moment of silence and then a few murmurs, the other executives in the room jumped in to own up to their own contributions while I watched the political volleyball from my seat next to Howard. He'd been back as ceo for two weeks, and the organization was aggressively working to get the business back on track after the stock price hit an all-time low.

I became the director of US Store Training in 2007, a time when things weren't looking so good for the business. The company had grown too fast in recent years, and the country was suffering from one of the biggest economic downturns in decades.

There was a nonstop effort to ensure the business hit its goals. The freneticism was both fun and stressful, but, by this time, Nick was almost four years old, and I felt like I could better manage the blended demands of work and parenting.

During this time, companies were laying off people left and right, and the housing market was flooded with new construction that sat vacant, creating ghost towns in formerly fast-growing areas like Las Vegas, Arizona, and Florida. People struggled to keep up with their mortgage payments, and banks were repossessing houses with a fervor. Starbucks had long positioned itself as an affordable luxury (treat yourself to a four-dollar cup of coffee even if you have to forgo that vacation this year!), but even we were not immune to what was happening around us.

Everyone inside the company was stressed and feeling the burden to right the ship. Wall Street analysts were questioning the long-term viability of Starbucks and poking holes in our balance sheet with a fervor. Desperate times called for desperate measures.

The corner of the eighth floor that housed the US business support team turned into a hive of activity. The fate of the overall company was at the mercy of the US stores, and if we couldn't turn the situation around, there might not be any more Starbucks. It was that bad.

Amid the constantly changing operational and marketing business tactics, the corporate functions and board of directors were also making tough decisions. One of the most significant was letting Jim Donald go from his ceo role and bringing back Howard Schultz as the company's leader.

Howard moved swiftly and with his usual passion and intensity, refocusing the company on a set of core priorities called the Transformation Agenda, intended to guide business growth priorities. He became highly visible, walking the halls of the Support Center to make sure people were all-hands-on-deck and weren't wasting precious resources. If the parking garage looked empty at 5:00 p.m., he'd send out an email questioning our dedication and commitment. More and more people showed up in the office on the weekends, filling the normally quiet building with the ambient noise of espresso machines brewing coffee and people collaborating on projects.

One of the newly stated Transformation Agenda priorities was to "realign and streamline the organization"—words that are a sure sign that cutting headcount is inevitable. Business leaders and teams did everything they could to make an impact and protect their teams and themselves by making tough decisions about projects and not backfilling open positions. No official announcement had been made that layoffs were coming, but you could sense it.

At the same time as we were looking at ways to cut costs, we were also looking for ideas to grow revenue. "Reigniting our emotional attachment with our customers and our coffee" was another Transformation Agenda point. And it was Howard's passion area.

The focus on coffee and connection (core values of Starbucks) had faded in the years leading up to 2008. Instead, all everyone seemed to talk about, and measure, was how fast customers were being served in the drive-through or how quickly they could be rung up at the register inside the store. Barista training content had morphed to match the business priorities and was now full of operational protocols and efficiency measures. Training baristas was expensive, and every minute was accounted for and had a dollar amount attached to it. There wasn't space for "nonessential" content, and most coffee education now had to happen on the job.

Upon his return, Howard became very accessible to the front line and listened intently to what baristas were telling him. They seized the opportunity to connect with him and openly wrote emails and letters about how they felt the company had lost its way. They described a shift in the company's priorities. Coffee and customer service, things that attracted them to Starbucks in the first place, no longer held the same level of importance. They said they missed the days when they could spend time with customers talking about coffee, and that there was too much focus on productivity. In their eyes, Starbucks was becoming like a fast-food establishment and losing its specialness. Store partners were growing disenchanted, presenting a huge risk to the business.

The notes from baristas lit a fire under Howard, and his well-worn path to and from the corner of the eighth floor was rerouted to the Training and Coffee departments. He wanted to understand how the company culture was being imprinted on new store partners and could be seen carrying training materials with him everywhere. He'd stop in offices and cubicles in a quest to find someone able to answer his questions about how past decisions were made.

Howard had been in his role as ceo for only a couple of weeks when he called a meeting about the Transformation Agenda in his boardroom on that dreary January day. He wanted to know what was being done, what innovative ideas were on the table, and who was accountable. He was specifically interested in how coffee quality and training were being addressed, given the outcry from store partners.

I was asked to join them due to my role as the director of US Training as Howard had purportedly heard from partners that they needed both more training and different training from what they were getting.

When I walked into the room, I said hello, glancing around at the executives already seated around the table. I immediately recognized that I had the lowest-ranking job title in the room, and, even though I had relationships with some of the others, I felt alone and vulnerable. I had no idea where this was going.

On the table sat the familiar shape of the barista training materials box in front of the chair that I assumed was Howard's. A small pit formed in my stomach as his assistant guided me to sit directly to the right of the open chair. My boss, Margo, sat on my other side.

Margo's usual high fashion was toned down, signaling that this was going to be a serious conversation. She normally pushed the edges of corporate dress code with stilettos, tight-fitting tops, statement necklaces, and flared jeans. For this meeting, she chose a long-sleeved, high-necked floral blouse and tasteful slacks. I think she was as nervous as I was.

Not knowing the boardroom meeting protocol, I kept quiet while the rest of the attendees filed in.

Howard came in last and sat in the spot on my left where I suspected he would. I peeked at what he was wearing out of the corner of my eye and took in his expensive-looking navy wool slacks. There was a fine maroon pinstripe woven through them, and he paired them with a simple, crisp white dress shirt and tan Italian loafers. He looked equally ready for the boardroom as strolling the streets of Milan on his way to dinner with friends.

Howard skipped introductions and the agenda, pointed at the training materials, and said the words that are forever etched in my mind: "Who created these? They look antiseptic. They look like they've been outsourced."

After I owned up to it, he continued with a nod. "Who changed the quality standards?"

He was referencing the milk steaming and espresso quality standards that had been changed to reduce waste a couple of years prior. I shared matter-of-factly that this was not my team's decision and that direction was set by the Coffee, Operations, and Quality departments. We merely captured the company standards and trained partners on them. As a training department, we rarely set policy or standard; we just taught how to achieve it.

I could tell that Howard was extremely disappointed, and I knew I was walking the fine line of throwing the other departments under the bus. But it was the truth.

He glanced down for a moment and shook his head to let the entire room know how he felt about these shortsighted decisions. From the very beginning, Starbucks stood by the promise of a personalized, high-quality, fresh cup of coffee, and now that was being compromised all in the name of profits. He held all of us accountable for not standing up for what was right. We were Starbucks partners, and that meant we were expected to act like owners of the company.

Curiously, no one in the room admitted to making the decisions, but everyone nodded feverishly in agreement that the standards needed to be changed back to what they were previously. The sense of urgency was heightened because the stores would soon be launching a marketing campaign claiming that we had the "best espresso in the neighborhood," something we needed to be confident we could stand by. The marketing campaign was the first major action in the Transformation Agenda since Howard returned as ceo; it was his chance to show partners, customers, and analysts he could get Starbucks grounded in its core values while innovating for the future.

Updating the barista training materials would be a major undertaking, so we focused first on the near-term priority of getting all US store partners trained on the original quality standards in time for the marketing promotion.

Usually, a project like this could take months, if not a year, but we had only six weeks to develop and deploy the training. The date for the marketing initiative had been set and communicated both internally and externally. There was a lot riding on this for the company and for Howard personally.

I had no idea how we were going to achieve this, which generated a swirling, crazy mix of intense feelings. The combination of exhilaration and sheer terror (I couldn't let this fail!) propelled me into finding a way to approach the work differently. Nothing could get in my way—the timeline was just way too tight.

The very first thing I did was assemble a small SWAT team of the best talent around me. They couldn't be just great training designers; they had to be innovators who were also organized and top-notch collaborators.

I cleared their calendars of all other work so they could focus only on this project, and I nicknamed them the Transforming Training team to remind them that their job was to innovate in ways that Starbucks hadn't seen before.

I created a "Bill of Rights" to hang on the wall in their dedicated conference room to remind them of their charter. Statements like "Do whatever it takes," "Don't take no for an answer," and "Have fun" set the stage for the culture I expected to guide this project.

I was relentlessly focused on freeing them up from the usual bureaucracy that came in our highly matrixed organization. We had only six weeks to get this done; there was no time for ad nauseam consensus or analysis paralysis.

There was so much work to do to make the training a success. The store espresso machines needed to be in top-notch condition. Some locations needed new steaming pitchers and supplies, and the technology in the stores to do any sort of training was severely lacking.

The former items were taken on by the Facilities and Procurement teams, but it was my team that needed to figure out how to deploy the training without a modern infrastructure. Every single partner on every single shift in every single store needed to be up to speed on the new standards before the marketing promotion launched across fifteen thousand stores in the US and Canada.

After a few brainstorming sessions, one of my direct reports, Shani, came up with the proposal to close the stores to conduct the training. It was a radical approach, and I was skeptical at first but was willing to entertain the idea because there didn't seem to be many other options.

Shani and I worked together when I was a regional sales manager in Business Alliances and she was a training manager. She came to Starbucks after a successful career in operations at Red Robin and had plenty of experience being scrappy and resourceful. She was a star at balancing creativity and pragmatism to achieve results and worked really well with others. Her voice wasn't always the loudest in the room, but she was a fantastic listener and could pull themes and pieces together that others might miss. You could almost see the inner workings of her brain making connections to disparate concepts while her gaze locked in on you as you were speaking. The occasional head nod reminded you that she was taking it all in and not drifting off to some other thought.

Shani advocated strongly to close the stores for training, confident that it would not just provide a higher level of assurance that store partners would go through the training, but that it could be a moment of connection. The way shifts were structured, it wasn't uncommon for store partners to never see one another, yet they still needed to operate the store as a team. Shani was always thinking about the culture and work environment, not just the project deliverables.

Closing the stores for training became our lead option, and we knew it would come up against countless obstacles, namely the expense to train everyone and the loss of revenue. But we were operating under the Transformation Agenda, and it was a new day at Starbucks. We were all being challenged to get back to our roots, instill confidence in partners and customers, and innovate in ways we hadn't before. And our proposal met all those objectives.

We just needed to make the pitch to Howard.

He had asked to meet with us for an update on the training because the marketing campaign was going to be one of the first highly visible actions since he'd returned as ceo. Training baristas would provide assurance to customers that we really did have the best espresso in the neighborhood.

Shani, Margo, and I waited outside Howard's office until we were summoned in. We had prepared a French press of Sumatra (his favorite coffee—it never hurts to grease the wheel) and conducted a quick rehearsal of our pitch.

When Howard opened his door and walked toward us with his usual look of intensity, Margo took a deep breath. "Here we go, ladies. Time to put our big-girl pants on," she said. There was no turning back now. We had to be as bold as the Sumatra we were carrying.

Howard invited us in warmly, and we settled on his cream-colored couch, the Seattle skyline occupying the view outside his windows. Margo opened the meeting while Shani began pouring the coffee. Howard wasted no time cutting right to the chase.

"So, what have you got?" he asked eagerly.

He was pleasant enough, but, in that moment, I was reminded that he was probably feeling ten times the pressure to deliver as we were. After all, he was trying to save his company.

We guided him through a pencil-drawn visual (he had a reputation for disliking PowerPoint) and explained that there would be three focus areas of the training: milk quality, espresso quality, and customer connection. He liked the simplicity of it and was in total agreement with the topics we proposed.

Then came the question we all knew was coming. "So, how are going to do this?" Howard was well aware that doing something of this scale and speed challenged our operating systems and practices.

I looked at Shani and gave her a slight nod. We had decided in our premeeting huddle that she was going to make the proposal to Howard, and Margo and I would back her up or take any heat. She was closest to the work, came up with the idea in the first place, and was very conviction driven about it. It was her chance to shine.

Shani remained as cool as a cucumber and kept it brief.

"We recommend closing the stores for a three-hour training. It's important to have every partner go through it at the same time to ensure they all get the training. It's also an opportunity to create a galvanizing moment for them to bond as a team."

Howard listened intently as Shani spoke, and then he quietly leaned back in his chair. We collectively held our breath for what felt like minutes but was probably only seconds.

A smile spread across his face, and then he spoke. "That's a big idea."

I sat there stunned. At first, I didn't think I'd heard him correctly. But when he started asking specifics about how we would do it, I realized that he was behind the idea. We were prepared for resistance, and instead what we got was carte blanche permission to make it happen.

Filled with giddiness and nerves, we practically ran out of his office, ear-to-ear grins spreading across our faces. When we got back to our part of the building, the rest of the team was waiting in eager anticipation to hear the outcome of our meeting. Margo shared the good news, and they roared and cheered enthusiastically.

Now it was time to get busy. We had a lot of work ahead of us, and time was our most precious commodity. Our renewed sense of focus and purpose fueled us. Nothing was going to get in our way of taking this thing to the finish line. We were not going to let Howard down.

The next days were filled with crazy long hours, and my family didn't see much of me during that time. The pressure to ensure this went well was immense but also energizing. Making a contribution of this level when the company was desperate and in need of invigoration was a once-in-a-lifetime opportunity.

On February 28, 2008, at 6:00 p.m. local time, all US stores were scheduled to close for the training. There was a big rally in the Commons at the SSC to involve office partners in the experience and let them know how they would be able to participate in the training. We wanted them to be connected to what the stores were doing and to understand why it was so important. It was as much about our culture as it was an operations initiative. We were all partners and had a shared responsibility to support the Transformation Agenda.

At 2:55 p.m. PST, we hushed the crowd and called into a store in New York to count down. When the clock struck 6:00 p.m. EST, cheers erupted through the Commons as every store on the East Coast locked its doors and began the training. Espresso Excellence was underway after six fast-and-furious weeks of hard work.

While SSC partners sipped their coffee, I shared a story about my own history with the craft of espresso when I worked at the University Village Starbucks as a barista.

The espresso bar sat on an elevated platform overlooking the store. This positioning was similar to that in the original Pike Place store, exactly like it was fifty years ago when it first opened its doors. I described the rigor and esteem that went into earning the right to work at the espresso bar, hallowed ground coveted by partners and revered by customers. The specialness of this position put it above all other roles in the store, and Espresso Excellence was bringing it back into focus.

That evening, I attended the training in my neighborhood store, eager to see it come to life.

I swelled with pride, watching the partners highly engaged and having fun swapping stories about favorite customers and their regular orders. Laughter permeated the air as they took turns steaming milk and ensuring they poured the perfect shot of espresso, letting one another critique their craft.

At the end of the training, they took down the chalkboard hanging on the wall behind the counter and wrote out the Barista Promise: "Love your beverage or let us know. We will always make it right." Then, with the chalk color of their choosing, each barista signed their name before hanging the board back up. A renewed energy and excitement for our future emanated from the store team.

The morning would bring a new day, a public declaration of Starbucks's recommitment to quality and service. We were now confident that we had the best espresso in the neighborhood. Period. And my team made it happen.

CHAPTER 9

When I was growing up, my cousin Sonja was like a younger sister to me. We were eighteen months apart in age and, as the two oldest kids in our group of cousins, naturally banded together during family gatherings.

She lived in a nice home with a closet full of cute clothes that I wistfully admired and wished I could fit into, but her willowy frame was at least two sizes smaller than my stocky body. I coveted a lot of Sonja's material things because I was poor and she was not, but she never made me feel inferior or lesser than. She shared openly and freely.

One of our favorite activities as kids was performing plays for the family. Sonja was always the princess, a blanket wrapped around her neck for a cape and a plastic crown perched atop her white-blond hair. She could master being both a damsel in distress and someone who could hold her own.

My brother, Jason, was cast as the prince, his dark hair and eyes a big contrast to Sonja's fairness. Bjorn, Sonja's little brother and five years younger than me, was told to portray whichever part had not been filled yet—baby, pet cat, or little girl. He did so eagerly, grateful to be part of our play instead of being shut out of the room during our rehearsals.

My role was always the director. I'd create a rough story line; tell the other kids what to wear, say, and how to move; and then narrate as needed when we performed for the adults. I was most comfortable being in charge, and the rest of the kids willingly let me lead because no one else wanted to.

We lived in Sonja's family's basement when I was growing up when my dad couldn't afford our own place to live, and I moved back in with her as a teenager, this time due to tensions at home with my dad and new stepmom.

After I graduated from high school and moved to Seattle, Sonja and I stayed in touch through regular phone calls and the occasional visit to see one another. Bonded like sisters, we found it hard to be apart, but we worked to stay connected.

After we each got married, we serendipitously got pregnant at the same time. Sonja was due two months before me, and I was relieved. She always knew she wanted to be a mom, and her calmness and pragmatism were just what I needed because pregnancy freaked me out. I was grateful that she experienced most everything just before I did because it took a lot of worry away from me. I could ask her a million questions about pregnancy, childbirth, and infant care, and she would share what she learned, offer advice, or just tell me to calm down.

Both of our babies came early, but still two months apart, and I continued to depend on Sonja's parenting mentorship. I missed having her closer and physically experiencing motherhood together, but we made an effort to visit one another so that our children could spend time together. We were eager to give them the time and space to get to know each other since they were not growing up together like we did.

When they weren't even a year old, we started talking about taking our children to Disneyland to celebrate their fifth birthdays. I hadn't been to Disneyland since I was a child and was excited to experience it with Sonja and our kids.

Our trip was planned out well in advance of the Transformation Agenda, but, when I started seeing the signs of what was to come at work, a sense of dread crept in.

In contrast to the positive energy surrounding the preparations for Espresso Excellence, every other project, process, and priority was being scrutinized. Each department was given an expense-reduction target, and mine was to reduce my budget by 20 percent and eliminate ten positions from my team of fifty. It was a terrible feeling to secretly plot someone's future without their knowing it, and the general unease in the building hampered productivity and ignited emotions.

Some people became gossipy and defensive, and nerves were jangled with anticipation of what was to come. Others were in denial and genuinely believed their work, job, and function would remain intact. Add to that the posturing and protectionism of corporate territories and a reluctance to share information among departments, and you had the perfect recipe for a toxic environment.

It all made it extremely hard to focus and keep team members positive, but that was the reality of the situation.

The senior leadership team had frequent open forums to transparently share the state of the company and the resulting call to action. They made it clear that if nothing changed, there would be no Starbucks in just a few short months.

With the Transforming Training team members squirreled away in their dedicated conference room with their Bill of Rights hanging on the wall, I was sequestered on the other side of the building, pulling apart my department project list and org chart. Our trip to Disneyland was in four weeks, and I was looking forward to a break from all the intensity at work.

Making people decisions was tough. I cared about each and every member of my team and their families and knew that any remaining partners would be asked to pick up the extra workload, and some might face "survivor guilt." It didn't feel like a win-win for anyone, but it was work that had to be done, no matter how painful.

In addition to the layoffs, some people would be demoted, and others would be offered new jobs in the company. Very few people were going to come out of this doing exactly what they had been doing before. There was no room for debate or negotiation in this process. All decisions were final. No matter how long someone had been with the company or how important their work was, no one was impervious to the implications of a company in survival mode.

The partner-notification date for layoffs was set and shared with vice presidents, and it was squarely in the middle of my Disneyland vacation. The rest of the organization was told that this would be coming in the next sixty days, but no exact date was shared broadly.

I was so torn—should I go on my vacation and leave the dirty work of the layoff notifications for someone else, or should I postpone my vacation so that I could be there in person to help my team through a difficult time?

I didn't immediately decide if I should stay or go on vacation and instead plunged myself into preparation mode for the individual team-member conversations.

A couple of weeks before the official notifications, I learned that my job would thankfully remain intact, but one of my peers was going to be affected. I had an inkling that she was going to be let go, and I felt guilty that I knew her fate before she did. This made me extremely uncomfortable as I went through the motions, working side by side with her, until the day her job was eliminated.

I decided to go to Disneyland with Sonja, my aunt Perri, Tate, and the kids but to do the layoffs via phone with the support of a Partner Resources person in the room with the affected partner. This wasn't ideal, but it was a way to respect those affected and honor the commitment I made to my family. Being a working mom meant trying to constantly strike the right balance with my priorities.

On the eve of the layoffs, I couldn't sleep. We'd spent a fun-filled few days meandering on Main Street, going on rides, and eating junk food. But that night, I lay awake, worried about how the conversations were going to go and the impact I was going to have on the lives of my soon-to-be former team members.

At five o'clock the next morning, I quietly let myself out of our motel room, careful not to wake my family. I shuffled to our rented minivan in the motel parking lot with a stack of termination letters and phone numbers for the partners I would be calling.

The warm California sun started to come up over the dashboard as I nursed a cup of coffee from a Styrofoam cup, choking down the green grassy flavor (the hotel lobby most definitely did not have a sign boasting "We Proudly Brew Starbucks").

I punched in the phone number of one of my managers on the East Coast, feeling sick to my stomach knowing the message I was about to deliver. I liked him and thought he did good work, but this was business. We were restructuring the organization, and all the positions at his job level were being eliminated.

When we hung up, I made the next call and then the next. After a couple of hours, my dirty work was done, and I was emotionally drained.

I gathered my things and stepped out of the minivan, squinting in the midmorning sun. My family was already at breakfast with Goofy, so I quickly changed my clothes and started walking toward the park. It was too late for me to eat with them, but I didn't want to miss the smiling faces of two five-year-olds who were having the time of their lives.

Grateful that I made the decision to do the layoffs myself *and* to go to Disneyland, I returned to Seattle and was thrust back into the throes of the Starbucks business crisis.

The Espresso Excellence training went off without a hitch the week after I got back, and I was so glad to have the layoffs and the training behind me. I could breathe again.

And then the wind was knocked out of me again when my grandma called.

"Chrissy, it's Grandma. I have some terrible news. Sonja has died."

My immediate reaction was disbelief.

"You're kidding, right?"

"Of course I'm not kidding. Why would I joke about that?"

I knew she wasn't joking, but I was in total shock. It couldn't possibly be true.

"She had a heart attack. John [Sonja's husband] called an ambulance and tried to resuscitate her, but it was too late."

I steadied myself against the desk in my home office and then slid to the floor. Every limb in my body was heavy with grief. She was a rock that had been a part of my life since we were little kids; with her death, I felt like part of me calved off.

It was surreal. I had just seen her two weeks prior at Disneyland.

I knew that she had been battling heart troubles and had been on medication for a variety of health concerns, but when I saw her on our trip, she seemed happy and like she was doing well. She was only thirty-six.

I dragged myself into our family room to share the horrible news with Tate. The world instantly became cruel and unrelenting. How could a life be taken way too early? How could a barely five-year-old girl have her mom ripped suddenly from her life without any explanation? None of it made sense.

I folded myself in Tate's chest, sobbing until there were no tears left. I had lost my best friend, my sister, and my counterbalance. Sonja was the calm to my storm, the light-hearted personality to my serious one, and the domestic goddess to my PowerPoint decks and bullet points.

And now she was gone.

CHAPTER 10

The grief and pain I experienced from losing Sonja waned slowly, but fortunately the company crisis of 2008 and 2009 faded quickly, and things were back on track at Starbucks, which eased the work pressure and stress I was under.

The previous two years, I had put my career on the back burner. I was in survival mode and took little time for myself—I was too busy worrying about and caring for everyone else. Figuring out how to parent an emerging grade schooler, laying people off with dignity, dealing with Sonja's death, and staying strong and steady for anyone who needed it took all my energy.

When things finally started to settle down to some sense of normalcy, it was time to invest in myself. My aim was to get back into Starbucks retail business where I started twenty years earlier as a barista.

In my role as training director for the US stores, I worked closely with the teams running and supporting the stores and loved the energy and hum of being connected to the day-to-day activity of the business. The relentless focus on the daily numbers, the constant exploration for ways to improve the store-partner experience, and the quest to innovate and delight customers was never-ending. The stores were the heartbeat of the organization and the sole reason everyone at the SSC existed, and I wanted to be a part of it again.

I started sharing my intentions with my vp, Margo, her boss, Jim, and whoever else could help me get back into retail.

I sought advice from people in Operations on what I needed to do to be considered a viable candidate for a field-based role and reached out to a vice president I knew, Sara, who had made a similar transition. Little did I know that she would someday become my boss and guide me to work with a career coach—the process that ultimately led to my resignation.

Sara and I worked together at the SSC when she was a director in Store Development and I was the training manager supporting her team.

She was one of very few people who had successfully made the unusual career transition from corporate to a field operations regional vice president role without any previous retail experience. She inspired others to believe that making such a move was within the realm of possibility.

With input from Sara and others, I decided that being a regional director of Operations would be the logical next role for me even though the jobs I had been in at the SSC were much broader in scope. This wasn't dissimilar to my career strategy when I was a training manager and decided to go into Specialty Sales and Marketing as an account manager. Both transitions involved taking a lateral move of lesser scope to gain overall breadth and experience, but, for some reason, there was less skepticism with this move. This was likely because the company had grown, and cross-functional assignments were more common. Plus, it was a great way to suss out whether I liked my new potential career track before I got in over my head.

Sara eagerly supported my career aspirations and graciously agreed to be my mentor. I attended one of her team meetings in Florida and spent a few days touring the market with different people on her team. When I got back to Seattle,

I continued my internal networking to uncover where I could learn and plug into operations team meetings and routines. It was all about positioning me as ready and relevant when the time came.

I knew up front that taking a regional director role meant that we'd have to relocate because the positions in Seattle were usually reserved for experienced operators, given the visibility and complexity of the market. Tate and I had a short list of places we would consider moving to—Colorado, California, Portland, and some East Coast cities—and it became a matter of waiting until the right match happened geographically.

Florida wasn't on our list initially—it was a far cry from the Pacific Northwest in terms of weather, geography, and culture—but we were attracted to the significant Latin influence in the southern part of the state. We had spent a lot of time in Central and South America and loved the vibe, language, and food. We contemplated a move to Mexico ten years prior, but we ended up taking our trip around the world instead. We put Florida on the "maybe" list but crossed our fingers that something would open up in a preferred location.

Six months after I started working my plan to get into Operations, Sara called to tell me that she had a spot for me on her team in South Florida. I couldn't believe that it was all coming together. My diligence and focus had paid off. Even though Florida wasn't high on our relocation list, it suddenly moved up to the top.

We decided to take a trip down there as a family to check out the area, including housing and schools.

Nick would be going into kindergarten in the fall, and we heard that the public schools in Miami-Dade County weren't that great, but private schools were superexpensive. This weighed heavily on our minds as one of the considerations for a prospective move.

Our late-night arrival from Seattle thrust us right into the vibe Miami Beach was known for. Ocean Drive was packed with fancy sports cars; dance music blared from the clubs; and there were throngs of people dressed in sexy party attire everywhere.

We exited the taxi at the hotel and were immediately enveloped by the warm air and ocean vapor as we made our way to check-in.

We went up to our room and ordered a pizza, starving because we hadn't eaten dinner even though it was 11:00 p.m.

While we waited on the balcony of our room for our food to arrive, Nick bounced off the walls with excitement, spotting the Ferraris and Lamborghinis on the street below. Throngs of people roamed the streets, caught up in the swell of energy boosted by music pouring from the dance clubs that lined Ocean Drive.

It hadn't even been ten minutes since we checked into our hotel room, and the whole family was caught up in the nonstop-party atmosphere of Miami Beach. We couldn't wait to get out and explore the next day.

There wasn't a lot of time to play tourist because our introduction to Miami was jam-packed with work-related activities, school visits, and neighborhood exploring.

On a housing tour with a real estate agent, we could already picture our lives high above the turquoise ocean in a unit with floor-to-ceiling glass, bright-white tiles and appliances, and tinted hurricane-proof windows like the places we saw on TV. Our Pacific Northwest earth-toned furniture certainly wasn't going to cut it in a space that screamed for chrome, glass, and white leather.

The condos were much smaller than our home in Seattle, but inventory was plentiful and move-in ready as the area was still recovering from the recession.

Instead of a front yard, Nick would learn to go down twenty stories to the condo complex playground if he wanted to be outside, and taking the dogs out for a potty break would be more complicated too.

But we could adapt to the smell of the ocean air coming in through the open windows, the expansive views, and the elevator ride to and from work and school every day. The picture of life in Miami was starting to take shape.

When we got back to Seattle, I told Starbucks that I accepted the offer—we were moving to Miami.

Sara asked me to keep the move confidential as they were planning to lay off a low-performing regional director and restructure the territory, so there were some unresolved moving pieces and parts. I secretly began to work on my transition and a succession plan for my job, unbeknownst to everyone on my team.

Other than moving to Seattle right out of high school, I had never lived anywhere else, so this move was a big deal. Sure, I had traveled the world and seen and experienced a lot, but uprooting my family was a whole different level of upheaval. The anticipation and excitement were high because we knew that the lifestyle and job would be in complete contrast to what we were leaving behind in Seattle. Prepping to downsize and move to a dramatically different climate meant that our winter clothes and skis went into storage, and Nick had to prioritize which toys he wanted. Bags and bags of stuff went to Goodwill.

Nerve-racking as it would be, the disruption in our life was one that we had been yearning for ever since we went on our trip around the world nine years prior. We just never imagined we would end up in Miami.

About a week before we were scheduled to put our house on the market, Rebecca, the Partner Resources director I had been working with on my relocation, requested a conference call to touch base about a few things. She wasn't very specific about the topic, but I imagined it had something to do with finalizing the communication plan because my move was still confidential.

"Hi, Christine. How are you?" she started the call.

"I'm good. We're getting excited about the move and have been busy getting the house ready to sell. We just need to figure out what to do for Nick's school in the fall."

"Well, there's actually been a change here. As you know, there're a lot of moving pieces with the partner that was going on a performance improvement plan, and the overall growth plans for the market have slowed due to the economy. We can still bring your family down here, but there won't be a regional director role for a while. You would come down instead as a district manager/regional director in training."

I was confused. Was there or wasn't there a job for me as a regional director in Florida?

"There will be a regional director job at some point," she clarified. "We just don't know when. Frankly, I think it's risky to make the move now because Florida was hit hard by the economic downturn, and I'd hate for you to come down here and then it be a year or more before a role came open."

"But what about the person on the performance improvement plan? I thought I was going to backfill her?"

"That was the original plan, but there are some new factors that have come up, and that change won't be happening for a while."

I wasn't surprised by her vagueness—Partner Resources peopled tend to be obtuse to protect confidentiality. But it still took me a minute to realize that there was no longer a director job for me in Operations in Florida. At least not in the foreseeable future.

Rebecca couldn't see me shaking on the other end of the phone, but she could probably hear it in my voice.

She had just told me that our move was off unless I would consider a demotion, and there was no time frame on when a regional director role would be available. The uncertainty of that was not an option for me, which meant we would be staying in Seattle until a position came open in a city that was a good match for both my family and for the company.

Tate and I were crestfallen. We weren't expecting this. All the personal business we had taken care of for this move needed to be undone—deciding on Nick's schooling, rebuilding Tate's business that he sold, and returning items we bought specifically for Miami.

Just when I thought I was finally getting off the emotional roller coaster of the previous year with the layoffs, Espresso Excellence, and Sonja's death, I plummeted down the most gut-swirling, unexpected vertical drop. I was already completely fried from all that I had dealt with, and now *this*.

My emotional and mental fortitude was cracking, and I needed a break before it broke me. I was tired, burned out, and frustrated. I had done everything I was supposed to do to prepare for a regional director role, and I was heartbroken. It was the straw that broke the camel's back or, in this case, my back.

If I didn't find some space to press the Reset button, I was pretty sure I'd fall apart. I declined the Florida district manager job and explored an extended leave of absence but wasn't eligible. I also considered a family medical leave, but I'd need a doctor's note indicating that I was unable to work due to mental duress, and I didn't want to go down that path. I feared a doctor wouldn't approve it and might think I was overreacting.

In my research, I discovered that Starbucks had a thirty-day personal leave option that could be used for any reason. While I was hoping for a bit longer than a month, anything was better than nothing.

Reset for me meant taking a mental-health break to pursue a passion, spend time with my family, and not think about or do any work. But what would I do and where would I go? And then it hit me—ever since we left South America, it had been a long-held dream of mine to take an intensive Spanish immersion course in another country. I was drawn to Latin cultures and had taken Spanish on and off since eighth grade.

I researched language programs in Mexico and focused on San Miguel, a quaint artist town in the hills five hours from Mexico City. I'd never been, but my mother-in-law had lived there in her early twenties, and her stories intrigued me.

I read that San Miguel, far from the beaches I had visited previously in Mexico, was a genteel colonial town with a large expat population of artists in residence. The climate was reportedly cooler than the coast, given the elevation, and much of the original architecture had been preserved and identified as World Heritage sites. It sounded like just the ticket—different from any place I'd been to before, yet with enough infrastructure to live comfortably for a month.

I found a recently renovated two-bedroom house for rent in a local neighborhood. Customary to the barrio, it was a two-story row house with shared walls and a courtyard in the middle that was open to the sky. There was a small deck on the third story where we ended up eating our breakfast every morning while our neighbor fried up fresh pork rinds on the adjoining rooftop.

Nick flew down with me, and we each enrolled in our respective Spanish schools with Tate planning to join us in a couple of weeks. I signed up for one-on-one instruction with a teacher named Sofia and looked forward to the twenty-minute walk from our house each morning. The school was in a bright one-story complex, decorated with Mexican folk art, and the classrooms surrounded an open courtyard.

My lessons were two hours per day, and Nick's all-Spanish summer camp was a half-day program, but he didn't last very long. He was overwhelmed by the cacophony of non-English-speaking voices and cried so much the first few days that I ended up pulling him out. Thankfully, Tate joined us earlier than planned, and he and Nick enrolled in a paper-mache art class while I continued my studies.

After my morning lessons, we would meet up for lunch and then take a siesta before heading out to one of the many parks to play or feed the pigeons.

Our routine included frequent stops at the local market around the corner from our house to stock up on oranges for fresh-squeezed juice and hot, homemade tortillas, which we ate for breakfast, lunch, and dinner. On weekends, we explored the local sights or paid the five-dollar admission to swim in the only pool in town, which was on the grounds of a hotel.

I relished my solo morning walks to school each day, meandering through the quiet tree-lined cobblestone streets and watching the city wake up. Most people were still at home eating breakfast and getting ready for school and work, their faces hidden behind the massive, beautifully painted and elaborately adorned doors and gates that fronted the streets. Those that were out were diligently scrubbing the sidewalks in front of their homes and businesses, the smell of soap fresh and strong. We exchanged polite nods and said, *"Buenos días"* as we passed one another.

I used my "commute" time to picture what I wanted my life to look like when I got back to Seattle. I wanted more time with my family, and I wanted to do work that was challenging and leveraged my strengths and passions. I wanted to take control of my career versus letting my career take control of me. And, even though Florida didn't happen, I still wanted to be in Operations. I was done being in a staff position that supported the business—I wanted to be part of the action.

I returned from San Miguel, refreshed and renewed. I was clear in my head and my heart about what I wanted from my career and from my life. I just needed to figure out how to make it happen.

As with my return from sabbatical and maternity leave, the only thing that seemed to have changed while I was gone was me. Work was work, but my perspective on my needs and priorities had both evolved and been confirmed during my time off. These breaks away from my job helped me see what I wanted and what was important to me.

I stepped back into my director of training role without missing a beat and quickly reimmersed myself in the priority projects. Not long after I returned, my boss, Margo, resigned, and I was appointed interim vice president of Global Learning while the search for her replacement went into motion. It wasn't the job I wanted, but there was a need, and I thought it would be a good opportunity to further flex my leadership skills.

I stepped into the role with confidence and as if the role were mine, never wavering in my decision-making and always maintaining a sense of command. But I knew deep down I didn't want the job permanently. I didn't let my ego get swayed by the job title or the stock options that came with it nor get influenced by all the encouragement I received to go for it. My heart just wasn't in it, and I knew that if I stayed in Global Learning as the vp, I'd be in the department at least two more years. I resolved to wait it out until another opportunity in Operations came my way.

As it happened, I didn't have to wait long.

The Operations Services department was pretty much as close as you could get to being in the field. The department designed and developed programs for the stores and was often the first point of contact for the majority of store issues and needs, from inventory to customer service to product delivery.

Most of the team was staffed with former district managers or directors.

I had gotten to know Craig, the department's senior vice president, through my work as the retail training director. He was my key internal client, and we had a positive working relationship.

Craig knew of my career aspirations and failed relocation to Florida and had been mentoring me informally over the previous year in my quest to get into Ops. His team was leading a huge project called Lean that was transforming the way work was done in the stores. He needed someone on the team who could effectively lead change and had excellent cross-functional working relationships. The director-level job he offered me on the Lean team wasn't in the field, but it was the next best thing. Plus, it would give me day-to-day visibility and interaction with the field operations team and the most senior leaders of the US side of Starbucks's global business.

I said yes.

We kept it a secret from the Global Learning team until two weeks later.

I joined my boss, Jim, in a conference room to tell everyone that I was not going to continue as their vice president. I knew pretty much everyone expected that I was going to be named the permanent leader of the department, given my performance over the previous five months. Espresso Excellence resulted in a lot of visibility, and the confidence with which I stepped into the interim role was more evidence to others that I was ready for the next level.

The room buzzed with anticipation, and people were laughing and talking when I walked through the door. Despite the joviality of the room, I felt trepidation leading up to the team announcement, hoping I wouldn't have any regrets about my decision. Many partners on the Global Learning team would be disappointed that I wasn't going to stay in the department, and I felt a little guilty, like I was abandoning them. They were craving stability and familiarity, and they didn't have a lot of confidence in Jim. But that wasn't up to me. I needed to move forward and work toward my goals.

Jim thanked everyone for being there and began to speak.

"I have an exciting announcement to make. First off, I want to thank Christine for the wonderful job she has done as the interim vp. I've gotten nothing but positive feedback on her from the leaders of the US business about the level of support she, and all of you, have provided them."

I looked out into the crowd and saw big smiles and expectant faces.

Jim continued. "Many of you know that Christine has a passion for operations and has enjoyed working directly with the business the last few years. Today I'm pleased to announce that she has accepted a role in Operations Services as the director of Lean Capability on Craig Russell's team."

The room fell silent. It was only a millisecond before people picked up clapping, but in that briefest of pauses, I felt their shock. This was not the news they expected to hear. I, on the other hand, was ecstatic. I tried to contain my excitement as I knew I would be leaving my former team in a less-than-desirable situation. There was no good succession plan, and Jim preferred to stay behind the scenes rather than be out front. He got nervous when thrust into the fast-paced needs of the business leaders. But he had the job title—and the accompanying salary—so it was up to him to figure out what to do next with the team. I was moving on and couldn't wait.

Even though I was passing up a vice president role for a lateral move, it was exactly what I wanted. Others were perplexed that I wasn't going after the bigger job, but that wasn't my motivation. I wanted a career change and to grow in new ways.

I stayed focused and didn't give up on my goal, even when things didn't go as planned.

Most important, I recognized when I needed to take a mental and emotional reset to ground myself in what was important to me at work and in life. This became my North Star when I returned from San Miguel to Seattle and the SSC.

And it kept me from doing what everyone else wanted me to do. I was forging my own path.

CHAPTER 11

When I first joined the Starbucks Lean team as a director, it was like landing in a new country, complete with its own regional jargon. My colleagues spoke the language of Lean, and although I could recognize a couple of words, I couldn't string a sentence together.

Their work norms were unlike anywhere else at Starbucks. The team embodied a culture of experimentation and iteration that contrasted with Starbucks's usual "just get it done and out the door as quick as you can" approach. The company overall had little patience for deep learning, even if it meant a better solution, which made it initially challenging for the really important work the Lean team was doing.

Lean is a method of continuous improvement that originated in Japan and is typically found in manufacturing environments. As it expanded into America, it found its way into other sectors, and Starbucks endeavored to streamline store operations to make the work easier for partners and improve service to customers. Everything from how a beverage is made to how a sandwich is warmed was looked at through a Lean lens.

Immersing myself into the group and into Operations took me back to Tate's and my trip around the world and what it felt like when our plane, train, or bus deposited us at customs and immigration—disorienting at first but eventually we figured it out. I worked hard to adapt to my new environment and study as much as I could about Lean and Operations. The learning curve was steep but fun. I was surrounded by highly intellectual coworkers with advanced degrees who seemed to have amassed some secret vault of Lean knowledge along the way. I had plenty of books to read, but my colleagues knew so much more than I did, and I had some catching up to do to fully contribute.

Their educational backgrounds and what felt to me like outsize confidence stirred my own insecurities because I never finished college. I had dropped out of school not long after I started working at Starbucks as a barista and never went back because it didn't seem like I needed to.

During my twenty years with the company, I had risen to the director level, and no one ever told me that my lack of degree was holding me back. I constantly reminded myself that I earned my way to my position just as much as those around me earned theirs. That said, being in Lean highlighted for me internally that I hadn't finished school. No one ever said anything to me; the stigma associated with not having finished college came entirely from within me. I suddenly felt more exposed with my lack of education.

In general, I tried to avoid talking about the college-aged years, but it always came up in conversation when I met people for the first time socially or in business. Introductions typically started with "Where did you go to school?" I usually gave a brief reply about why I dropped out of school and then quickly changed the subject. College was a big part of many people's life experience and identity, but not for me—I felt secretly awkward and incomplete.

Deep down, I wanted to go back to school someday, but it never seemed to be the right time. There were always plenty of reasons not to: demands from work, family commitments, finances, the fact that I already felt accomplished in my career without a degree. No matter what, there was always an excuse.

When the stresses of life in 2008 and 2009 came and went, I realized that if I didn't go back to school soon, the day might never come. I was forty years old and wasn't getting any younger. It was very unlikely I would suddenly have less on my plate and more time on my hands before I retired, and I didn't want to wait that long.

When I started pulling apart the barriers, I realized that there weren't any that couldn't be solved. I could pay for school with my Starbucks stock, and I could establish some boundaries around work-related email and hours spent in the office. Tate and I made the big decision that he would be a stay-at-home dad while I was in school and working full-time to ensure Nick had a primary caregiver. I quit my book group and kept personal care as a priority with any available discretionary time. It definitely wouldn't be easy, but it was doable.

But my biggest barrier was believing in myself. As much as I wanted to finish my degree, I was scared I might fail. Not in the literal sense (I knew I wasn't dumb), but I was scared that I might not be able to handle the stress and time commitment and would have to drop out.

I easily decided that I needed a classroom experience versus online. I couldn't see myself sitting at home or in a coffee shop, plowing through a curriculum on a computer. I needed a sense of community and people to talk to, and being in a classroom would also help me with accountability and focus.

I looked at several colleges in the Seattle area and ended up choosing Antioch University, a small liberal arts school that had a bachelor's completion program geared toward people like me—full-time working adults with some life experience under their belt who were looking to either better their job prospects or learn about something that interested them while finishing their degree.

The other major benefit about Antioch was that they offered the opportunity to get credits for my work experience that could help me close my credit gap more quickly. The credits weren't automatically awarded (there was an extensive process that included writing a syllabus and a white paper to support the demonstration of prior learning and experience), but it would speed things up because I could work on proving those credits while also attending classes.

I chose leadership and organizational studies for my area of concentration. It was an easy selection, given it was relevant to my job and I found the subject matter interesting. I grew up at Starbucks and had seen leadership from pretty much one perspective my entire career, so I was eager to expand my understanding.

It took a few months to find my rhythm of being a student, employee, mom, and spouse, but I eventually settled into a routine. Sometimes I would come home for a quick dinner of turkey tacos before I went to school, while other nights I ate at my desk at work right before I headed to class.

It was hard not seeing much of Nick during the week because he was often already in bed when I got home. Tate and I crammed in couple time when we could, but school was a big rock we had to work around. It wasn't uncommon for me to arrive home at 10:00 p.m. and fall into bed hard, exhausted from the long day, only to get up at 5:00 a.m. the next morning to do it all over again.

Despite a very full and demanding schedule, I loved going to school. Most of my classes were interesting, as were the professors, but it was the other students who made my two years at Antioch so enriching.

The majority of my colleagues at Starbucks were college educated, and the workforce was pretty homogenous, so the diversity Antioch exposed me to was not what I expected from a college experience.

Very few of my classmates were from the corporate world, and the cultural and ethnic diversity in my classes created a melting pot that I hadn't experienced before. Being in this new cohort stretched my understanding of society and leadership constructs in new ways.

There were a few students whom I had multiple classes with during my time there, and they became an important part of my experience. Julia, a Muslim woman, planned to open a private school for Muslim girls, which is now thriving. Denise went back to school to further her career in health-care administration and has since received her master's degree. Shep had a long career in insurance but was hoping to get into real estate as he transitioned into midlife. Jessica spent much of her career in theater and the arts, finished her BA at Antioch, and is now working toward her PhD in education. I loved being around all of them as what they brought to the table was so different from my business context.

The two years flew by, and before I knew it, graduation was just around the corner.

* * *

One of my final requirements for graduation was to do a capstone project designed to bring together my entire BA completion experience. There weren't many guidelines on it because Antioch had a philosophy of encouraging independent thinking. Selecting a subject was up to me.

I decided to create a leadership model that was an amalgamation of my twenty-plus years of experience as a leader. I had drawn off so many different frameworks in my career that I had evolved my own unique approach to leading and developing people.

I was often sought out for coaching and leadership advice from coworkers across the organization, and I relished these requests because I was passionate about helping people elevate their leadership approach.

However, my ideas and teachings were a jumbled list of concepts anchored in a medley of the various principles I'd been exposed to over the years. Although I was a skilled practitioner, my approach was all in my head, and when I tried to convey my wisdom in a simple and actionable way to others, I got flustered and couldn't clearly articulate the secrets to my success.

With my outline in hand, I shared my senior synthesis project proposal with my school adviser, Carson. I told him that I wanted to create a leadership model called Nemawashi Leadership.

Nemawashi is a Japanese term I learned in Lean that literally means "cultivating the soil so the tree will grow." I felt that concept was analogous to my approach to developing people—taking the time to care and feed, having patience, and adapting to the elements all eventually produce a healthy and strong plant (or person). I was excited to start building it out and incorporating what I learned while at Antioch.

"This is good," Carson replied. "I think it will resonate with people."

He was supportive of the idea but encouraged me to push it even further.

"I'd like to challenge the purpose and reason for your senior synthesis. You said you want to make a leadership model, but I think your project could have deeper intentions. I'd like you to consider making your project less about creating a model and more about focusing on the process of taking what is implicit to you and making it explicit. Your classmates and community will benefit from you sharing why that has been hard for you up to now and how you've developed this skill through this project and your time at Antioch."

At first, I didn't get what he was saying. I felt like he was redirecting everything I wanted to do. Then I realized he wasn't suggesting I throw out the model, but that I expand on *why* and *how* I was creating it in the first place.

All my life I've done what I've known best as a manager and leader, experimenting with different ideas and then keeping what worked for me. I'm a sponge with a thirst for knowledge.

But when it came to explaining or teaching what I've done and why, I fell mute. Boasting about my accomplishments made me extremely uncomfortable. Years in training and development and sales had ingrained in me to listen more than I talk, even if talking meant helping others. I used questions to facilitate insight in others as my primary coaching practice, so much so that along the way, someone gave me the nickname "master asker."

As I listened to Carson's recommendation, it dawned on me that Antioch's educational philosophy wasn't just about making sure students graduated with the requisite number of credits—it was about cultivating personal growth. A thoughtful senior project should be reflective of my *experience*, not just the content.

The whole benefit of going back to school suddenly clicked into place. It was so much more than getting a degree. It was about expanding my awareness of the world, my community, and myself.

Putting pen to paper and organizing the model proved overwhelming at first. Getting what was in my head out in some fashion was initially scattered and disjointed. I was just getting started and could already feel the stretch to take what was implicit and make it explicit.

I captured my jumbled thoughts on Post-it notes lining my desk at home and filled a journal with notes from interviews I conducted with people who had worked with me in the past. I probed for their perspectives on my leadership style, listening not only to the words they said but also to the emotion and energy with which they described me.

I extracted insights and learnings about community and political leaders from my studies and began to see connections to my own leadership style that I hadn't seen before.

One leader I was particularly inspired by was Abraham Lincoln. I didn't pay much attention in US history growing up, but I had the opportunity to get extra credit for one of my classes if I read *Team of Rivals* by Doris Kearns Goodwin. I devoured the seven-hundred-page biography about Lincoln's leadership style over a single weekend (I was recovering from a newly broken ankle thanks to a ski accident, so what else was I going to do?) and used many of the stories as points of reference in my senior synthesis.

I was inspired by how he leveraged the strengths of those around him, like when he appointed William Seward as secretary of state and Edward Bates as attorney general even though they were initially interested in other cabinet roles. He could see what they each uniquely brought to the table and how this would benefit the whole team.

Eventually, these inputs were captured in a visual depiction of Nemawashi Leadership, a circle divided into four named quadrants: Authentic, Intentional, Cultivating, and Community-Building, with a heart in the center of the model titled "Helping." I believe being of service to others is the foundation of leadership, and being in the center connected it to the four quadrants. A leader's job is to help people learn and grow, recognize when they can't do it alone, and help paint a picture of hope for a compelling future.

With my first draft of the model done, it was time to get to the heart of my assignment: teaching it to others to see if it was an effective tool that represented my leadership beliefs while at the same time, clearly articulating the process I went through to get there.

Initially, I was embarrassed to shop it around because I feared it wouldn't make sense or that I would sound full of myself talking about what had worked for me. I started sharing it with those I interviewed for the project, and, when the positive affirmations came back, I started to relax. I got more comfortable making the implicit explicit and could see that the content in the model resonated with others. It seemed I had a story that they gravitated to.

The last step before graduation was to present my Nemawashi Leadership project at a forum called the Senior Symposium. It was open to anyone in the Antioch community and my invited guests.

I asked my Starbucks team and a few other colleagues, including my boss and former boss. Nick and Tate also showed up, beaming with pride and bearing an armful of flowers for me.

Dressed in my most flattering light-gray pantsuit and my new diamond earrings that I got as a graduation gift from my family, I walked into the large conference room with nerves swirling in my belly.

There were about twenty guests milling about, eager to listen to my presentation. I felt like I was the bride at a wedding as I made my entrance, greeted everyone individually, and thanked them for coming. The room overflowed with love and support.

Stepping up to the podium to begin my presentation, I felt at ease, and my feelings of vulnerability faded when I saw everyone in their seats smiling back at me. It clicked in me that this was it—after this presentation, I would finally be a college graduate at age forty-three. Overcome with emotion, I let a few tears of joy seep out of the corner of my eyes. I was so incredibly proud of myself.

I pulled myself together and started my presentation. I could tell how closely everyone paid attention while I spoke. They stared at me intently, smiling and taking notes. Thirty minutes later, hands shot up in the air for the question-and-answer period.

As I wrapped up the Q&A, I thanked everyone for being there, and the room erupted with applause. I was relieved to be done, sweat seeping through my suit jacket.

I think going back to school as an adult and with twenty years of work experience was meant to be for me. If I had stuck with it right after high school, I wouldn't have made the relevant connections to real life or been able to put my learning into practice right away. Conversely, I wouldn't have been able to bring my daily work into the classroom to synchronize theory and practice.

I was becoming skilled at ignoring the tug of the "shoulds" and instead, listening to my natural instincts about what was right for *me*.

Forging my own path over a more conventional one was emerging as a theme of my life.

CHAPTER 12

School was initially a huge change, but ultimately felt relatively manageable in my director role on the Lean team. I had fewer direct reports than when I was in Global Learning and had just one big project versus a bunch of smaller ones.

Our charge in Lean was to improve the work processes in the stores to make it easier for baristas to do their job, improve customer service, and improve productivity.

I was brought onto the team to ensure the program fit into the company culture and didn't come across as too mechanical or factorylike. If it didn't get rolled out in the right way, it ran the risk of not only being rejected by partners, but also being misunderstood by customers, the public, and possibly even Wall Street.

There was company enthusiasm for this initiative, as well as a lot of pressure and expectations, but the team was committed to its success and believed it would be a game changer.

At the time I came to Lean as a director, the vice president was a man by the name of Joe. He previously held a strategy role at Starbucks but became inspired by the work Toyota had done to improve efficiency while simultaneously creating a culture of problem-solving and employee involvement. He made a pitch to Starbucks senior executives that the principles of Lean could be transformative for the company, even though Lean had never been implemented in a food-service or retail environment before. Unlike a manufacturing organization, we had customers walking in the door while the work was being done, adding a layer of complexity when trying to create a culture of continuous improvement.

Fueled by his passion and a vision, Joe did some trial experiments that proved the applicability to Starbucks, and the Lean team was born.

It took a while to get the leaders of the organization on board as the concepts required deep learning and a new way of leading. There was skepticism that Lean could deliver business results, and some had a hard time seeing past the technical rigor required. The initiative, called Playbook, required constant education at all levels in the organization and clearly wasn't something that could be rolled out in a day.

Because the work was for the stores, keeping operations leaders informed and engaged was critical. It was going to impact them and their organizations the most, and they needed to be prepared to lead the change. With an initiative of this scope, we needed their buy-in and ownership for Playbook, because if it ended up being perceived as nothing but a corporate mandate, it would fail. Even a glimmer of doubt could sink the whole project. The stakes were high.

About nine months into my role as director of Lean, we were nearing pilot expansion, and our team had the opportunity to provide an update on Playbook to the operations vice presidents. We broke them up into groups and led them through a hands-on learning exercise because we felt strongly that they needed to experience the degree of change that was coming to the stores so that they could start to internalize what would need to shift in their own coaching approach.

When everyone reconvened in the main meeting room to debrief the exercise, Joe took them through a presentation on the business case and implementation plan. As he spoke, I could tell things weren't going well. All I remember is an air and feeling of discontent as the presentation unfolded.

Side conversations started happening, and the question-and-answer portion of the session was getting out of hand. It was not good. I stood in the back of the room, watching nervously and trying to figure out what was going on. The field operations leaders were always tough critics of initiatives coming from the SSC. And they needed to be—they were the ones who had to live with all the hairbrained ideas that the corporate offices came up with.

The presentation wrapped up. Later that day, I walked by Joe's office and noticed he was talking with his boss, Craig, having what looked like an intense conversation behind the closed door.

Outside, the team huddled around each other's cubicles, trying to dissect the meeting and figure out went wrong and what was going to happen next. We waited with bated breath for Joe to come out and debrief us, but he stayed in there for a very long time. It was close to 6:00 p.m., so we resigned ourselves to packing up for the day. We would have to get an update tomorrow.

A couple of days later, there had still been no communication about the meeting, but the tension in the air was palpable. We were in an awkward pause, unsure if the project was moving forward in its current state or not. We tried to stay focused, but it was distracting not knowing what to do next.

At the end of the week, I was reviewing some Lean training materials when Craig's assistant came by and told me that he wanted to meet with me in a half hour. She didn't tell me why, or why the meeting was in a conference room across the building versus his office.

I felt sick to my stomach—having secret meetings far away from my work area was what I did when I laid people off. Was that going to be my fate?

When I walked in, the head of Partner Resources was sitting next to Craig, and my heart immediately jumped into my stomach. I noticed that Joe wasn't there, though, and I tried to piece things together. Just a few weeks prior, my only direct peer in our work group had been fired, and anxiety within the team had been high since that occurrence and the operations vp meeting.

If layoffs weren't imminent, the only other thing I suspected was that the project was being killed. I started questioning if I made the right decision moving to this team and this job in Operations. Would I have to go back to the career-plan drawing board?

My pulse raced as I sat down in the chair, with Craig and the head of Partner Resources to my right. For those first few seconds, it was hard to focus as I looked around nervously, my gaze landing briefly on the posters featuring the latest coffee promotion. I noticed that the conference room blinds were closed so that any curious passersby couldn't see who was in the room—another tactic when conducting job elimination conversations.

Craig got right to the point. "Christine, we wanted to let you know that Joe is no longer with the company."

He offered no explanation before he continued. "We'd like to offer you the vice president job backfilling him. You've demonstrated strong leadership and have built trust with the key leaders, and we have all the confidence that you'll be able to take Playbook and Lean where it needs to go."

I did not see any of this coming. Here I was being promoted from director to vp to lead a function where I lacked technical experience and had been on the team for less than a year—I was flattered . . . and scared to death.

My head swam with worries about my recent return to school. I had been at Antioch just six months and was finally starting to feel my groove. Could I maintain it all with the added pressure of a vp role? What would this mean for what little time I had with my family already?

There was no way I was going to quit or put school on hold again after all these years. It took a lot of courage, a major family decision, and my own hard-earned money to see it through, and I was committed, no matter what.

I genuinely thanked Craig for the opportunity and told him I was honored but that school would remain a priority. Craig patiently listened to me. When I was finished, he smiled and said, "That's why you need to have a great team."

He was right. I could do it all. I just needed to surround myself with the best talent and create an environment for them to do their best work. I said yes and immediately plunged into my new role.

Being an executive in charge of a function where I had limited subject-matter expertise was daunting. I hired an external Lean coach to help me, and the rest of my training for my new role happened on the job. There was no time to immerse or ramp up—we had huge, highly visible deliverables coming at us like a fast-moving train.

Nothing prepared me for the weightiness of being vice president and having the buck stop with me. Decisions about people, financials, and work-plan priorities were all now in my court. This was the most significant change from my director job, and it overwhelmed me. I worried I might make the wrong decision, but I knew that kind of worry came with the territory of an executive role. There was a higher level of risk and reward at this level. I was keenly aware of that, and it was reinforced on my very first day as a vp.

I was in a meeting with a couple of team members and Scott, one of my new peers, discussing some data and facts about a project we were working on and that we needed to decide whether to take forward.

Scott had come to the SSC from a regional director role in the field, and we had worked together the last few years. He was a nice guy who approached things with a genuine curiosity and a ratcheted-up level of intensity, which could be a little unnerving if you didn't know him well. His regular CrossFit routine put him in tip-top shape, his hands rough with calluses while everything else about him was perfectly pressed, likely a carryover from his days in the army.

The matter at hand was very time sensitive, and there wasn't the opportunity for my usual deliberativeness and need for additional background. We had to determine in that moment whether we were going to move forward with a project that I knew very little about. I generally tried to heed my own leadership advice of "fake it till you make it," but this was one instance where I didn't feel like faking it would benefit anyone. I needed more information, but I knew there wasn't time to gather it.

Everyone in the meeting room got quiet and looked at me, waiting patiently for me to share my point of view. I felt paralyzed—what if I made the wrong choice? Scott could see me sitting there in discomfort, silent and pondering. Without hesitation, he looked me straight in the eye and said, "It's your decision."

I practically looked behind me to see whom else he could have been talking to, but, of course, it was me. And I knew he was right—it *was* my decision. I suddenly felt woefully ill-equipped for the job. That familiar feeling of insecurity and self-doubt set in. I was beginning to wonder if it would ever go away.

Would being a vice president require that I make big decisions impacting employees, customers, and the business on a regular basis without what I felt was enough information? I would soon find out that the answer was yes. I was faced with situations like this every day, and, while I gradually got more comfortable with it in practice, I always secretly wished I had a little more time to research the background. I became a master of faking it till I made it.

About six months into my role, I became acutely aware of my insecurities in the position when it was time to sit down for my annual performance appraisal.

Craig was moving into a new job, and he and my incoming boss, Rossann, felt it was important to have a check-in conversation together with me before they transitioned. I appreciated the conscientiousness of this leadership decision and their desire to create continuity with a well-thought-out handoff.

Rossann and I knew each other from her previous role as a Field Operations senior vice president, and she had a stellar reputation for developing people because she deeply and genuinely cared. Her passionate intensity and direct communication style could be off-putting if you didn't know her, but her intentions were always positive. She mentored a lot of people and always made time for you no matter your role.

As a leader at the table, Rossann had a way of cutting through the crap and the overt political maneuvering to get the business and her colleagues focused on what mattered most. She led strongly and compassionately with a point of view that advocated making the job easier for store partners.

In the Monday morning US Leadership team meetings, she tended to sit back and listen with composure and then jump in at the end with a very strong opinion, which brought the whole room silent, and usually into agreement.

Rossann was taking over Craig's role because he was moving into the Global Coffee department. Her Starbucks tenure incorporated a variety of job rotations in the field, including a stint when she led the Europe, Middle East, and Africa team in Amsterdam. Coming to the SSC was for her own development, even though she was vocal about her distaste for the building. She hated bureaucracy and felt that there was a lot of waste at corporate and that certain resources could be better directed elsewhere.

Craig, Rossann, and I were huddled around a small conference table in Rossann's office, which was crammed with bookcases full of leadership books, a few mementos from her career, and, in the corner, her small roller bag that she toted to and from home each day.

I took in her outfit, which was consistent with her usual style: tailored pantsuit, crisp colored designer dress shirt in a hip pattern, fashionable eyeglasses, and stylish but comfortable shoes. Her curly grayish hair seemed to have a life of its own, naturally slightly unkempt, a contrast to the rest of her ensemble.

Craig and Rossann opened the conversation by letting me know that I was doing a good job and had transitioned into my role smoothly, especially given the circumstances. They each shared that I had effectively stabilized the team and moved the work forward while building credible relationships with the business leaders.

After a few minutes of positive feedback, they then turned it over to me to share my own perspective. I skipped over my accomplishments and immediately rattled off all the things I still needed to learn in the next six months to up my level of contribution.

The list was long.

I was far from a subject-matter expert and still saw myself as a junior company executive. I explained that I was ramping up and couldn't really tell how long it would take me to feel confident and competent in my role, but that I was doing my best. In the back of my mind, even though I had earned the position, I felt secretly that someone might out me as a fraud.

Rossann sensed my feelings of insecurity and suddenly interrupted me midsentence as she peered over her glasses.

"So, you think you haven't made it yet?"

She must have seen the frozen look on my face, because, before I could respond, she continued. "You *have* made it. You are an executive officer at a Fortune 200 company. You got this role because you earned it. Stop doubting yourself.

"Also, when you start every sentence with 'I'm still learning,' it can shake others' confidence in you. Remember how you got here and that you *are* here now. Now, stop saying, 'I'm still learning' all the time."

I could feel my face flush at her directness, and I wasn't sure where to go next in the conversation. I was also momentarily confused. Starbucks had been teaching us that a growth mindset and demonstrating curiosity were essential skills for leaders, so when did learning become a bad thing?

After a minute of processing her feedback, I realized that what she was really getting at was owning my position and demonstrating confidence. It wasn't about me *not* learning, because I'm always in learning mode—it's part of my core being. It was about me not constantly *talking* about still being in learning mode. She was reminding me to draw off the experience, wisdom, and knowledge I had gained over the years and to be resolute in that. I wasn't expected to be a master in my role, but I had plenty to contribute; otherwise, I wouldn't have been promoted.

Without realizing it, I had been forgetting to practice what I preached. I often coached others to "fake it until you make it," but my own method was just the opposite—more like "learn it and then you earn it."

The pressure I put on myself to knock it out of the park right out of the gate (not unlike when I first went into Specialty Sales and Marketing years prior) was unrealistic, and I needed to pause and acknowledge what I had accomplished. And if I didn't know how to do something, I could always draw off the experience of others.

Rossann's comment jolted me, but I knew she cared more than anything for me to be successful and keep growing.

I took her feedback to heart, and the conversation with her and Craig served as a major pivot point for me. I *was* a vice president and earned the role. From here on out, I was going to own it full on.

Over the next few months, there was a noticeable shift in how I approached problem-solving and decision-making. I walked taller and held more command in the room. My executive presence went up a level, and I used my newly found confidence to press forward with Playbook implementation with a new level of energy.

From that point forward, when I felt a moment of uncertainty, I reminded myself how I got to where I did and, if needed, told myself to "fake it till I make it." The more confidence I portrayed, the more successful I would feel and appear, and that success bred more confidence.

I knew faking it wasn't being inauthentic, because I already *had* made it. I was an executive officer at a Fortune 200 company.

CHAPTER 13

My peers and I were in a meeting with our new boss, Michael, about the proposed organizational change we were to announce to the broader team the following morning. It did not go as expected, and I walked abruptly out of the room and hurried to my office, seething with anger. I felt railroaded in the meeting and as if my voice and opinion were irrelevant. I was embarrassed that all my ideas had been shot down in front of my peers, and, in that moment, it became crystal clear that the leadership values I believed in were more important than agreeing with my boss.

I couldn't believe what I'd just witnessed from a senior vice president. For a company that prided itself on a relationship-oriented culture, his autocratic and dictatorial style was in direct contrast to what I had known during my twenty-plus years at Starbucks. I was caught in the eye of a leadership storm, and I didn't know how to get out.

It was 2012. Starbucks had survived the economic crisis of 2008 and 2009 and was feverishly finding ways to reinvent itself and maintain relevancy with consumers. New products were being added in the stores at a rapid clip, and the company was acquiring other companies in an effort to extend product lines and create new ones.

There was a tremendous amount going on with the acquisition of Teavana and the La Boulange bakery chain. On top of that, Starbucks Blonde Roast and a new product using green coffee extract called Starbucks Refreshers were introduced to the stores. It was hard to know what the true company priority was.

My job had expanded to vice president, Business Optimization, during a time of immense change. My team had just started introducing Playbook to the field in the hope of adding structure and standardization to help absorb all these new products in a time of rapid evolution.

After less than a year in the role, Rossann moved on to a new job inside the company, and I got my third boss in less than eighteen months. This was not unusual for Starbucks.

My new boss, Michael, came into his role with an enthusiastic fervor and energy. He had been with the company for a while and had spent years in fast food and the quick-service restaurant business before joining Starbucks.

His background and experience gave him a high degree of credibility, and his gregarious nature and affability made him a very likable person. Before he became my boss, we had known each other from his role in the field, and I'd seen his direct East Coast style in action. He wasn't shy with opinions or his love of a good debate.

It was a lateral move for Michael, and, like all executives new to a role, he came in like a force, expected to demonstrate results quickly. At Starbucks, the first ninety days are all about quick wins, and failing to demonstrate them could stunt your career. It was like hopping on a speeding train with the goal of getting to the next destination as fast and safely as possible without the train derailing. If you didn't make an impact quickly, you risked being left behind.

Michael set up an immersion plan for himself, getting deep into everyone's work and meeting with other senior executives to get their perspectives on where his department was performing well and where they had concerns.

Given the resources associated with my organization and Playbook, and the expected results, there was understandably a lot of interest in what we were up to. I approached Michael's curiosity with full transparency, sharing where I felt we were solid and expressing where we needed help.

One of my biggest concerns was the simultaneous implementation of warmed food being introduced to the stores along with Playbook. We couldn't risk overlooking the increased complexity of work for the baristas out of excitement at having flaky, French pastries hot out of the ovens.

That said, even if this meant more work for the stores, partners and business leaders were excited about the upgraded quality and charmed by La Boulange's romantic story and expressive, passionate founder. Not only would the product be a lot better than the food currently offered, but there was an expectation it would deliver significant sales growth in a stagnant category.

The US leadership team, comprising Operations vice presidents and above, met in San Francisco to get ready for the launch. Between manufacturing tours and visits to La Boulange cafés to absorb the ambience, we gathered in a conference room in the basement of a downtown hotel that had been transformed into a gallery of ingredients that went into the pastries.

Conference tables overflowed with fresh strawberries; long, thin bars of dark chocolate normally stuffed inside croissants; bags of high-quality, fresh-milled flour; and cubes of rich European butter. Other tables were adorned with fresh flowers and draped in French fabrics with stacks of mouthwatering

sweet and savory baked goods and towers of caramel and chocolate sauce jars to take home.

I was listening intently to one of the presentations on our
first morning of the meeting when I noticed an email notifi-
cation on my phone from Michael. I was curious as to why he
would be sending it to me when he was sitting just two tables
away. I clicked Open.

The subject line read "Confidential: Do Not Share with
Anyone." It was addressed to me and copied to the most senior
executive responsible for the US business at the time.

My stomach lurched as I read paragraph after paragraph
describing his dissatisfaction with the work my team was doing
on Playbook. He made it clear that he thought our implementation approach was all wrong; there were too many resources
required, and it was taking far too long. He told me in his email
to stop the work immediately and redesign the entire program
and implementation plan, including scaling back on training,
and to launch it in pieces and parts instead of the whole system
as designed.

I sat there in silence, trying not to let on to those sitting
at my table that I was completely rattled by his message. He
closed the email by reminding me that I wasn't to share it with
anyone—this was only for me and the senior executive he copied on the email (which I assumed at the time he did to get his
support). It was clear from his tone that I needed to follow his
direction.

I was suddenly in a very difficult position and felt stuck
with no way out. It was clear there was no room for discussion.
This was a directive, and the only apparent option was for me
to execute his orders.

I felt backed into a corner, not just with this project but
with my career. I feared that if I didn't do as Michael said, he
would make it difficult for me to get advocacy and support for
future positions and projects in the organization. On the other

hand, if I did do what he asked, I'd have to get my team on board to move in a direction I didn't believe in myself. This was one scenario I couldn't fake until I made it.

I was fuming and tried hard to stay present the rest of the meeting, but I couldn't help turning the scenario over in my mind to see if there might be other options. I glanced over at him sitting a few feet away. He was acting as if nothing had happened, so I decided to do the same, at least on the outside. Dealing with this would have to wait until we got back to Seattle.

* * *

Back at the SSC, I tried to brainstorm some other ideas with Michael, but he wouldn't budge. The head of the US business even came by my office to acknowledge the email from Michael and wanted to get my opinion on the directive. I told him confidently that the original plan we laid out was the one I believed in, and I explained why. I could see he was perplexed. He'd been a champion of our original direction, but now he was likely dealing with some added political maneuvering due to Michael's arrival. While I hoped my conviction would influence him, I knew that I'd have to wait out the hierarchical machinations.

For now, I felt stuck and knew I was going to have to muscle through this working relationship. As Margo said right before we walked into Howard's office to propose shutting down the stores for Espresso Excellence training, it was time to put my big-girl pants on.

I respected Michael's request to keep the email confidential and did not share his direction with anyone. Tate provided an outlet for me at home to express my frustration, which he responded to with his usual soothing and unwavering support.

At work, I sought advice from other leaders and advisers to get their opinion of my team's work as well as on how to work effectively with Michael. It was a delicate situation because there was risk that I might sound whiny, inflexible, or thin-skinned.

My reputation was clearly more at stake than Michael's. He was at a higher executive level than me and was brought in to shake things up. If Playbook didn't go well, it was on me. And if he didn't like the current direction and got everyone else to believe in that too, that was also on me.

In a company where partners were supposedly the center of the universe, titles, hierarchy, and positional power were how things got done at Starbucks in recent years. This contrasted with my early days with the company when all voices were heard without blowback or consequence. Michael's seniority mattered in modern-day Starbucks, and the true voice of the partner often got lost in politics at the executive level.

I tried to talk with him about it, but he was resolute. I kept my relationship with him amicable but felt a constant level of strain underneath. I was frustrated by his inability to truly seek to understand and listen to those around him, and I was annoyed that when he finally did ask a question, he didn't wait for an answer. He'd jump right in with a five-minute monologue followed by the consummate rhetorical question, "We're good, right?"

To be clear, Michael wasn't a bad person—just a terrible "boss fit" for me. I was doing my best to muster through the situation, but the thread I was hanging on was getting thinner and thinner. I was losing sight of who I was and what I stood for as a leader, and it didn't feel right.

I continued ahead, doing my best to lead my department, trying to find middle ground with Michael and manage my emotions. I clenched my teeth and tried not to overreact when he went around me to provide direction to my team, instead saving my resolve for more-worthy battles. I took a deep breath when he canceled my trip to China because he said he was more senior and hadn't been there yet, so I needed to wait until he went first. I played nice and focused on problem-solving in meetings with him and my peers instead of being outwardly irritated.

It perplexed me that someone could rise to this level of leadership in our organization with limited collaboration and listening skills. It made me question my own leadership style, and I felt myself constantly wondering if I needed to act like him to succeed at Starbucks.

Then, one day, it all came to a head, and I realized I couldn't take it anymore.

After he'd been in his role about six months, Michael decided he wanted to look at our organizational structure to maximize efficiency and ensure we were equipped for growth.

I had a lot of experience designing and implementing organizational structure changes because they seemed to happen about every eighteen months at the SSC. I agreed with him that we should look at how we were getting our work done, given the company's shifting priorities.

I was tasked with holding some ideation sessions with team members and was to return with a final structural recommendation to present in the next couple of weeks. It was a group effort, and I met with the team several times, also having conversations with my peers and the Partner Resources manager to work out some options and ideas. In the end, we came up with a high-level plan that we all agreed upon and that I would share with Michael when we reconvened.

The night before the Town Hall (an all-department meeting), we secluded ourselves in a conference room far from our work area so that we could have some privacy and avoid curious walk-bys. My peers, Michael, and I needed to walk out of that conference room with some decisions made, because we were committed to sharing a refreshed department vision and evolved organization structure at the Town Hall the next day.

The broader team knew something was coming; they just didn't know what. Any hint of a potential organizational change created uncertainty for what the future held and resulted in speculation and anxiety. They didn't know that we weren't charged with cutting headcount or laying off anyone, but they were bracing for anything.

After we all sat down, I passed out copies of the recommendation to everyone and walked through our decision-making process and why we believed this was the best direction. We had established design criteria, highlighted problems to solve, and proposed some modifications to the existing structure.

Throughout my presentation, I could tell right away that Michael wasn't listening. He was fidgety and looking around the room, not at the document in front of him.

When I wrapped up reviewing the proposed structure, I asked the group for questions and feedback.

Without hesitation, Michael jumped up from the table and went to the whiteboard where he sketched out an alternative organization. Not surprisingly, it was *completely* different from what I had laid out.

"This is not what I expected. It's way off base," he said, pointing to the PowerPoint document that outlined the structure our working team created.

"The new org needs to look like this." He gestured to his illustration on the whiteboard.

None of it made sense to me because it combined functions that were dissimilar, and the new workflow looked like it would be more complicated. That said, my peers all nodded in agreement with him, either because they liked his recommendation better, or they didn't want to rock the boat. In truth, they probably just wanted to wrap up the meeting and go home. It had been a long day.

My blood boiled. I was apparently the only one visibly not in alignment, even though I created the better recommendation with members of the team, a couple of whom were sitting right next to me.

However, not only did Michael disagree with it; his swift sketch on the whiteboard had me wondering if he already had something in mind before he even handed me the assignment. He'd obviously been thinking about it and knew what he wanted, which didn't match at all what my working team proposed. I started to question the real motive behind the task to create an org structure that was going to be cast aside. The make-work of it all infuriated me, and I felt like I did in that hotel meeting room in San Francisco a few months prior when I got that "do this, but don't tell anyone I told you to" email—backed into a corner.

I had reached a tipping point. It wasn't just the org-structure project; it was the cumulation of situations I experienced while working with Michael. I didn't expect him to agree with me all the time, but I at least wanted dialogue and collaboration to help me problem solve and learn.

I was angry and felt undermined. Rossann and Craig had coached me not long before to own my position, and I felt like Michael was taking ownership of it instead. I had slid from a confident, seasoned vp to someone who felt useless and unworthy of the job title.

I scooped up my materials with shaky hands and left the meeting room without speaking. It was after 6:00 p.m. at this point, and I had arrived at the office at 7:00 a.m. I could feel myself cracking from exhaustion and emotion. I needed to get out of there as soon as possible.

Cooling off enough to get my head wrapped around demonstrating support for Michael's org model in front of our one-hundred-person team the next morning was going to be hard because I had no ownership over the decision.

I stopped by my office to grab my coat and was pulling my office door closed behind me, my whole body vibrating with anger, when Michael came barreling around the corner.

"Christine!"

I could tell he knew I was upset, and I had a feeling he was coming to make amends of some sort, but I was too steamed to have a rational conversation.

I turned around sharply and yelled down the hall, "Don't talk to me right now! If you do, I'm going to do or say something I'm going to regret!"

For the first time in my career, my usual steady composure lapsed, and I didn't care. This was completely out of character for me, but I was tired of playing the game. I was not going to let someone walk all over me.

I turned around and marched away from him, not looking back. I needed to calm myself down before I did something drastic like unleash a torrent of unkind words or even quit in the heat of the moment. The cumulative months of constant, incessant talking without listening, direction without collaboration, and action without discussion had pushed me over the edge.

A quick glance at him out of the corner of my eye told me he knew he had made a mistake—I could see it in his face.

Once settled in my car, I unleashed the stinging tears I'd been holding back into a faucet of angry sobs as I leaned against the steering wheel.

I wished so much Tate were home to give me a much-needed hug, but he and Nick were fulfilling a bucket-list trip skiing in Chile. It was August in Seattle, which was the middle of the winter south of the equator, so it was the perfect way to spend summer vacation.

When I got home, I Skyped them, and they could immediately see how upset I was—my face was puffy, and my eyes were rimmed with red. I was beside myself trying to hold it together, but they could see right through me.

Tate was compassionate and supportive, and I could tell Nick was a little worried about Mom's meltdown. I assured them I'd be okay as they gave me a big virtual hug from thousands of miles away.

Tucking myself into bed after we hung up, I contemplated staying home from work the next day to give myself some distance from the evening's mess. I really needed some headspace to figure out what I was going to do next, and I was embarrassed by my outburst in the hallway. In my mind, vice presidents should be tough and composed and not let themselves fall apart.

But I needed to show up for the next morning's Town Hall to reveal the org structure and give the team confidence in our future direction, even if I personally wasn't buying into it. I settled into a fitful sleep, determined not to let this situation completely knock me off the rails.

I dragged myself to the office with bags under my eyes and the best attitude I could muster and got up on the stage to show the team that I was a leader committed to them. They weren't aware of what happened the previous evening or that I didn't see eye to eye in general with our department's senior vice president. What mattered most was that I was there to support them through this transition. I owed them that.

From that point forward, Michael and I were civil to each other for the duration of our working relationship, but I knew that couldn't last. He may have been set in his ways, but so was I, and I needed to find another spot in the organization where I could operate more autonomously and where my input and ideas were valued.

If I learned anything from my time working with Michael, it was that I needed to persevere, stand up for what I believed in, and lead in a way that was authentic to me. I'd been down that path before. My trek in Nepal taught me how to persist amid extreme difficulties, and living in Mexico for a month to study Spanish centered me on what was important in my life.

I knew that if the opportunity didn't present itself to me organically while I was working for Michael, I'd eventually need to go find it.

My wish came true a couple of months later when Michael unexpectedly bounced into my office to share some exciting news.

He did frequent pop-bys, but this time there was a little extra swing in his step, given what he was about to reveal.

He shared that Starbucks was going to be doing a global leadership conference, and I was the preferred internal vp candidate to lead this very high-profile two-year project, reporting to the office of the ceo. There were several other contenders, but I had a strong chance.

Starbucks leadership conferences were held periodically to bring store managers together for inspiration and education, to set a vision, and to lay out a call to action. Designed to be highly experiential and emotional, programs in the past included big-name celebrities like Bono and Alicia Keys, although Howard Schultz was the true main attraction for partners. He and members of his team were intensely involved in design and development, and it would be the first time they were putting a full-time vice president on the project.

It was an opportunity of a lifetime, and I was honored that I was among those being considered.

Michael most assuredly sensed that I was unhappy and probably knew that a change would be good for both of us. I thanked him for telling me about the project and told him I'd like to put my hat in the ring.

Two weeks later, I was chosen for the role.

This leadership storm had passed.

CHAPTER 14

The term "midlife crisis" conjures up images of women dressing too young for their age and silver-haired men kitted out in leather jackets and chaps on their new Harley-Davidson motorcycles. Stories of marriages falling apart when the kids go off to college because couples don't know what to talk about anymore are not uncommon either.

Even though it's not an official mental-health disorder, enough research has been conducted to establish that, sometime between the ages of forty and sixty, people may experience depression and/or the need to make big changes because the end of life is getting imminently closer. This has come to be known as midlife crisis, and I didn't want to have anything to do with it.

Instead, I coveted midlife *clarity* when I reached my late forties.

That was what I called it anyway.

In truth, it probably wasn't all that different from a crisis; it just manifested itself differently. I yearned for clarity about what was important to me and how I could deliver value, be valued, and love what I do.

I was feeling a little lost and a lot of restlessness, and I wanted to take control of my future, instead of letting it take control of me.

Nick was in middle school, and I could see that it wouldn't be long before he'd be out on his own. Tate had settled in as the stay-at-home dad and had unequivocally supported my career aspirations and commitments. But I wasn't sure *what* I wanted anymore.

I never thought I would retire at Starbucks, and I certainly never even had a vision that I'd be there over twenty-five years. I just was.

Deep down, I knew that finishing out my working years there was not how I wanted to live the next decade of my life. I just wasn't sure what was next.

When I started as a barista, it was because I needed the $5.40 per hour to pay rent, and I'd heard that Starbucks was a good company to work for while going to college. My career trajectory at Starbucks far exceeded anything I imagined, and, by the time I left, I was one of only a handful of executives who had started out with the company slinging espresso.

I always knew I wanted to do more with my life and can still hear my aunt Perri's voice telling me how on top of it I was as a kid. I was the one corralling the cousins, planning the group activities, assigning roles, and then directing everyone accordingly. Because of this, my family predetermined that my life would take me down the path of either a politician or a businessperson. I definitely didn't have the patience for a political life.

These character traits stayed with me into adulthood, and although the long-term vision for my life wasn't crystal clear, working in business and constantly seeking out new challenges was always in my sights.

While I was lost in my search for midlife clarity, recruiters from Fortune 500 companies constantly contacted me for senior leadership positions where I would have positional power and a nice fat compensation package.

It became clear at this stage of my career that if you were at the executive level but weren't moving up the ladder, it was because you were on your way to retiring.

Neither ladder climbing nor early retirement were in the cards for me, though. That wasn't my aspiration. I wanted to work, but I needed to have purpose and meaning while doing so.

I was on my fourth vice-president job at Starbucks when I felt a shift inside me that something was missing. I wasn't having as much fun at work anymore.

My one-year assignment on the global leadership conference came to an end, and I transitioned back into Operations as vice president of Customer Service and Operations Services.

The work was fulfilling, but I began to develop a bit of restlessness, not unlike the feelings that precipitated my previous sabbatical and my month-long stay in San Miguel. I was craving change, but I didn't know what I wanted to do next.

I was reporting to Sara (we had come full circle since my prospective move to Florida), and she did her best to guide me but could tell I was stuck. She decided to support me with an external coach at Starbucks's expense, and I was relieved and grateful to have someone help me through the process.

And thus began a four-month-long career-exploration with my career coach, Susan. I dubbed it my Midlife Clarity Project.

At our first meeting, I was a little skeptical that she was going to be a good fit for me, given that she came across as formal in her conservative skirt suit and high heels, a stark contrast to our casual office environment. Her makeup and hair were spotless, and she carried a briefcase with a digital writing tablet she used to keep her client information organized.

I was initially a little intimidated by her presence and was pretty sure that her typical clients were in higher-level positions and more sophisticated than me.

I was already doubting myself, and we hadn't even gotten started.

Once Susan and I started chatting, I began to relax. She was genuinely interested in me, my story, and my aspirations and was easy to talk with. She listened intently as she scrawled notes on her device and often interjected with affirming comments like "Wow, that was a significant project" or "You must have been frustrated when that happened." It became very clear early on that she was there for *me*, even if Starbucks was footing the bill.

For the first time in ages, I felt like I had an objective supporter and cheerleader to help me move my dreams forward with no strings attached. I didn't have to worry that my candor with her would impact my future career with the company. She was my advocate and trusted adviser, often pumping me up and helping me recognize all that I had accomplished and what I had to offer.

I had no idea if our work together would mean I would stay at Starbucks, or if I would end up leaving. All I wanted was to see where the process took me, and to emerge with a crisper way to describe what I wanted to do and a clearer roadmap for my future. That was what success looked like for me.

And so, together we undertook an intensive exploration of my background, values, strengths, and personality traits.

She interviewed me several times to not just learn my job history but also to observe how my energy peaked and valleyed when I described my past. These conversations illuminated a set of patterns that she confirmed with a battery of style and work-preference assessments she had me complete.

Deep down, I was also a little worried that the data might possibly reveal that I was a fraud and not worthy of the job scope I had. Insecurity reared its ugly head again, and I was starting to wonder if I'd ever get over it.

I grew up at Starbucks with no real perspective on what it was like to be an executive in another company and often wondered if I really was at the same level as peers in other departments and companies.

The conversations with Susan and the assessments I completed debunked those myths that had wedged themselves deep into my brain. Instead, she extracted some very positive themes, and my confidence gradually increased as a result of the process.

The final phase of our work together was spent conducting interviews with leaders at Starbucks whom I'd worked with. With their input, we would further unpack my unique abilities and find out their perspectives on my weaknesses.

I identified a half dozen trusted peers and senior leaders who knew me well and could provide a diverse array of honest opinions.

Customarily, Susan would have conducted these interviews, but I asked her if I could do it instead. I could tell by the subtle shift in her body language that this was an unusual request. We talked through the pros and cons of my doing it versus her, and ultimately, we decided that it could be a great opportunity to enroll others in my journey while deepening relationships. The only risk was there might not be the same level of transparency as there would be if Susan conducted the conversations, but we thought it was worth a try.

I was anxious going into my first interview, which was with a direct peer of mine. She sat across from me in my office with a big smile on her face, which immediately put me at ease. I started with the easier questions, which were about what set me apart from others in terms of my skill set. Her response surprised me. I had no idea that one of my unique gifts was the ability to move large bodies of work across the organization effectively while making everyone feel involved and valued.

My second interview was with the president of the US business, someone I liked and respected and with whom I had a good relationship. His influence on my career and my future was weighty, so I was a bit more nervous meeting with him than the others.

Not surprisingly, he was present, engaged, and happy to see me spending time getting clarity. He immediately expressed that my ability to continuously learn and grow impressed him. He mentioned that he thought this was highly unusual for someone who had been in one organization for so long and that I demonstrated an ability to lap my own performance, which was extremely hard to do in a fast-growing organization.

I was scared to ask the next question because it would reveal his honest opinion about my place in the organization from the highest levels: What would he *not* turn to me for?

He replied without hesitation. "I wouldn't turn to you to lead a group in crisis or in an urgent business-turnaround situation. Your strengths in deliberation and collaboration could get in the way during a time that needs decisiveness."

Hearing this hurt, but I knew it was true—I'm not comfortable in rapid-response situations. I like to take my time and do the research before making a recommendation or implementing a plan of action.

The rest of my interviews yielded similar themes, and even though I felt highly vulnerable and exposed, it was good to get it all out and to start to see a story form. The pieces of the puzzle to my future began to fall into place.

At the end of the four months, Susan gave me a very simple document that laid out what she saw as four criteria for my perfect role: serving others (internal or external customers), leading teams, implementing projects and programs on a very broad scale, and having a boss who complemented my style but was not too tangential from the department strategy and priorities.

She suggested that, when these elements were in place, I'd be at my highest level of performance and engagement. Now I just needed to find a job that matched.

Buoyed by these new insights, I met with many of the top leaders at Starbucks. People seemed genuinely interested in helping me match my strengths and passions with the company's needs.

In a couple of instances, I went out on a limb and put myself out there for roles that might have initially appeared to be unconventional choices, given the work I'd done in the past.

None of these came to fruition, but at least I started letting people know where I saw myself adding value and where I didn't.

Enrolling others in my quest to find a meaningful job at Starbucks was both energizing and deflating. I was itching to get going and at the same time, couldn't see an immediate path forward.

Tate kindly tried to help me see that, even though I had put a lot of energy and time into my midlife clarity project, it would take time for others and the organization as a whole to catch up to my new goals. He reminded me that it could be months before something opened at Starbucks (or elsewhere for that matter) and to keep my expectations in check.

I appreciated his perspective and attempt to ground me, but I was done being the long-term partner who had become a plug-and-play utility player in the organization.

Being a utility player was flattering for sure, but I felt like I was a passenger in a car, at the whim of my driver, and not in the driver's seat.

Over the years, I had taken on a lot of different roles because of influence from others: Need someone to lead a new high-profile team of functional experts called Global Business Optimization? Plug in Christine. When the department vice president quits and the senior vice president doesn't have credibility with the business, who can be a respected temporary bridge? Plug in Christine. What do you do when the Store Development department doubles in size to get ready for increased store count and the current training manager isn't performing? Plug in Christine. And so it went.

Being a utility player gave me great leadership agility and breadth, and I was often recruited internally by other departments because of my broad skill set. It was nice to be wanted and wooed, but sometimes I felt pressure to take positions that didn't necessarily light my fire.

My midlife clarity project with Susan put me in the driver's seat from there on out. My next role, whatever it was, needed to be what *I* wanted and needed. I was determined not to settle for less than what I believed I deserved.

After six months of searching internally, I started to get discouraged and felt my energy and momentum waning.

My future at Starbucks ambiguous, I began to wonder if I was finally at the end of my ride after twenty-seven years.

CHAPTER 15

You know how it is. There's a certain path in life we are supposed to take that starts with going to college right after high school so we can get a good job someday.

After that, we're on our way to a "real" career. Meanwhile we struggle to pay our bills and rent with a low-paying, entry-level job. Eventually we have some years behind us at work and might even become a homeowner or meet a life partner along the way.

Sound familiar? It may not be everyone's reality, but it's a customary route many people take along their way to midlife and then retirement.

My path wasn't so different, even with its unique twists and turns. I stayed at one company for twenty-seven years. I married Tate when I was twenty-six years old. I socked away a good nest egg and didn't veer off in any dramatically different direction.

But when my midlife clarity project with Susan didn't yield any job prospects at Starbucks, I decided I needed to take a closer look at what I wanted out of the next phase of my life and career. I didn't care as much about financial security anymore and what I was "supposed" to do—it was time for me to do what I *wanted* to do.

I couldn't responsibly quit my job to further my soul-searching, so I applied to take another sabbatical from Starbucks. My boss, Sara, had been with me lockstep on my work with Susan, so she wasn't completely surprised by my request, but she also knew that getting it approved was another matter.

I wanted to start it in just two months so that I could maximize the summer with my family and then return after the holidays. Not only did my request not meet the usual requirement of six-months' notice; there would also be a need to quickly create a plan to cover my work while I was gone.

But the real potential sticking point was that executive sabbaticals were secretly frowned upon, even though it was a bona fide benefit. It wasn't explicitly communicated, but I knew culturally that sabbaticals taken by executives could be perceived as demonstrating a lack of commitment because we were expected to show up day in and day out and be available all hours of those days. Alternatively, sabbaticals were sometimes used as a cover for leaders on their way out of the organization, never to be seen or heard from again.

I didn't care how people perceived it; I felt like I needed it more than anything. My previous sabbatical was precipitated by an itch to do something radically different, whereas this one was more about finding fulfillment and living my values.

I crossed my fingers that Sara would be able to push it through, which she did.

Even though I had some objectives for my sabbatical, those first few weeks off felt strange. I wasn't accustomed to having nothing on my calendar and felt anxious and unproductive living life in the slow lane. I was conditioned to back-to-back days that started at 4:15 a.m. and ended at 9:15 p.m. just so I could pack it all in—gym, work, and family time—and I initially felt compelled to replicate that crazy schedule during my leave of absence.

To ease the discomfort of too much idle time, I had a list of prospective time fillers in the note app on my phone. It contained things I fantasized about doing when I had more leisure time and included things like hiking, picking blueberries, and exploring Seattle parks I hadn't been to. With Nick (now thirteen years old) out of school for the summer, I couldn't wait to spend a lot of my free time with him.

Two weeks after I started my sabbatical, Nick had already had enough of my crazy calendar of activities. I was running over my ideas for the week ahead at dinner one night when he looked right at me and, in a matter-of-fact way that only a teenager can deliver, said, "Mom, don't ruin my summer."

He obviously had a different idea of how summer should be spent, but I had never bothered to ask. I was too worried about letting it slip through my fingers because who knew when I'd get another summer off while my kid was still living at home.

But what Nick was really telling me was that the pace of game on my sabbatical didn't need to be the same as it was while I was his full-time working mother. He was giving me permission—and a direct order—to relax.

Heeding his not-so-subtle request, I took a different approach to my days from that point forward. I stayed focused on what I called my "big rocks": community service, time with family, and training for the New York City Marathon.

When fall rolled around, Nick was back in school, and it was time to start digging into my midlife clarity project and ramping up my marathon training. Even though Starbucks wasn't paying for Susan's services anymore, she graciously provided me with some direction.

I decided to focus my exploration on the health and wellness industry because I was attracted to the idea of helping people feel better about themselves physically and mentally. I believe that a healthy well-being enables people to show up and contribute in a positive way, making them more present and available to others. When we are in pain, it's hard to do this, and the resulting isolation propagates more pain, literally and figuratively.

I knew this from personal experience when a running injury temporarily ripped me out of my running community.

I didn't start running until late in life, inspired by Nick's participation in a running program when he was in the fourth grade. Their after-school training culminated in a 5k race, and I decided to sign up as well, figuring that if my ten-year-old could do it, then I could too.

Running outside intimidated me for some reason, so I did all my training for that first race on the treadmill. It may have been because I didn't think I was as athletic as the runners I saw wearing leggings and fast-looking tennis shoes, huffing and puffing around the lake near my house. They looked like they were in a different league from me, and I had no idea if I had the right form or even if I was putting one foot in front of the other like they were.

I had a blast at the 5k and eventually got the courage to try running outdoors, only to discover that I loved being outside so much more than in the confines of my gym. It gave me a way to explore my neighborhood differently while breathing in fresh air and experiencing a greater variety of terrain.

I eventually gave up the treadmill completely when I found a running group after a search on Google. I was increasing my early-morning miles and wanted company for safety while it was dark out. It took bravery, but I showed up at a Seattle Green Lake Running Group Meetup at a neighborhood Starbucks at 5:30 a.m. on a rainy February morning for a loop around Green Lake even though I didn't know a soul. I was nervous and hoped someone would be my friend and not judge my lack of experience as a runner. I found a few people running at my pace (even though I didn't really know what my pace was yet) and hung on to them like an eager puppy, not wanting to get left behind.

In time, I became a regular and started showing up on Saturday mornings and then Friday mornings too. Friendships formed fast over the miles and created a level of intimacy unlike other social groups I was a part of. There's something about settling into a stride and not looking at one another that breaks down barriers and creates a level of trust. An hour or two goes by, and before you know it, you've disclosed your deepest desires and anxieties to a near stranger.

Within a few months, someone in the group convinced me to sign up for a half marathon and, two years later, my first full marathon. I was inspired by the encouragement I received from my new friends and someone once telling me, "If you're going to run one marathon in your life, make it New York." I secretly registered without telling a soul, and when I was accepted onto the American Heart Association team, I raised almost $10,000 in honor of Sonja and crossed the finish line, heading into the arms of Tate, Nick, and Sonja's daughter, Kalina, a huge smile on my face.

I battled persistent knee issues on and off, but I'd found a wonderful sports chiropractor at the recommendation of one of my running buddies. Sure enough, I had a severe IT band injury. My running routine was put on hold for a couple of weeks until it had a chance to recover through rest, treatment, and rehab.

I could live without the physical aspect of running for a short time, but I was most devastated by not seeing my friends. We spent hours together each week, providing nonjudgmental support and a willing ear, and having this outlet disappear, even temporarily, was going to be difficult. This group had become my sanctuary away from home and work, and now there was a big hole in its place.

My experience with the running group and subsequent injury sparked my interest in the health and wellness industry. If I could be a part of a business or organization whose mission was to spread positivity, community, and healthy living, I would be able to impact more lives in the way mine was impacted.

At first, I didn't know where to start because Starbucks is a very insular company and little value is placed on maintaining an external network. There is also virtually no time to do so during a sixty-hour work week, so for me, networking meant flexing a new skill.

Susan suggested I use my sabbatical as an opportunity to learn about what was happening in the health and wellness industry to see how my skills and experience might translate. It wasn't so much about looking for a job at this stage in the game, which alleviated pressure on me as well as on the people I was looking to meet with.

I was surprised at how willing people were to connect with me. They were superinterested in Starbucks and my experience, given the positive reputation of the brand and my tenure with the company. They wanted to hear *my* story as much as I wanted to hear theirs, and my confidence rose a notch with each meeting. Through these conversations, I started to realize how much value I could bring to a variety of organizations, confirming that I had plenty of skills and experience to offer and that people wanted them. They wanted *me*. They were curious as to how I rose through the ranks of such a well-respected company and how I adapted at each phase of the company's growth. As they related their own organizational challenges with talent management and scaling operations, they were eager to hear my ideas on how to do that well while keeping culture intact.

Each conversation started with an inquiry about their own personal story before I launched into questions about their industry, competitors, and strategy. I followed that with curiosity about what made a leader successful in their space and what challenges they faced in serving their customers.

It was all about positioning myself as a thoughtful peer and business executive, not as a job searcher.

One of the people I met during my sabbatical networking efforts was the ceo of Tangelo Manual Therapy + Movement, the place that rehabbed my injured IT band. Like many founders and small business owners, Mike was extremely passionate about his business, but he was even more passionate about the award-winning culture he'd shaped for his company.

The service his team provided me was outstanding, and I felt successful through my rehab, never embarrassed at being a newbie runner who lacked knowledge and experience. There was constant positive reinforcement of what I was doing and how I was progressing, with plenty of education along the way.

Each time I walked through his clinic door in Seattle's Green Lake neighborhood, I was greeted with smiling faces calling my name. High-energy music pumped overhead, and I'd get a high five and a "Bye, Christine!" from the whole staff at the end of each appointment.

Beyond the exceptional service, the physical design was completely different from a typical sterile doctor's office. There were no cheap prints hanging on the walls or fake plants in need of a good dusting. The space was built with half-wall partitions for the doctors to treat clients, offering some privacy but filling the space with light. The lack of closed-door offices also enabled communication and camaraderie among the staff. Everyone was smiling and seemed so positive. It was unlike anything I'd experienced in a typically clinical setting. I was very curious about Mike's secret sauce and aspirations for growth, so my doctor facilitated an introduction to him, and we set up a time for coffee.

At that first meeting, Mike exuded the genuine positivity and passion I experienced from his team. Practically every other word out of his mouth was "culture," and, from my experience as a client, I knew that his company lived up to its values. They were painted on the walls in each of the three locations and in the corporate office, to let clients know what they should expect and to remind team members what they were held accountable to.

Mike's insatiable curiosity was unfurled in a stream of questions, and he listened intently to my answers. I could tell that continuous learning and self-development were important to him and that he liked to be around people who stimulated his own thinking.

The energy between us flowed easily as we envisioned ideas for the future, talked about industry problems that needed solving, and brainstormed different ways to grow his business. I didn't have any health-care experience, but I knew what worked and didn't work from a client perspective, and I thought he had something special.

I was inspired by his vision, and our complementary skills and symbiotic set of values became evident early in the conversation. We each believed serving people—both our teams and our clients—guided our purpose.

Before I knew it, our planned sixty-minute conversation ended up being ninety minutes. I left that first meeting excited about the possibilities to drive change, and we agreed to stay in contact.

I spent a few months having similar exploratory conversations with others, but I couldn't stop thinking about Mike's business. I could clearly see the potential for his company because no one in the industry was doing what he was doing the way he was doing it, and I envisioned the value I could bring to him and his team. My skills in scaling up as well as my experience as a seasoned leader and coach could help make his dream a reality—he needed someone like me to grow his business to fifty locations and beyond. More important, I liked him as a person and believed in what he stood for.

As excited as I was by our conversation, I tried hard not to get too emotionally invested in the idea of working with him. He didn't have an open job, and going to such a small company would likely not be feasible for me compensation-wise. I was the primary breadwinner in my house and had a lot of equity and great benefits at Starbucks. Making a radical change at this phase of my life seemed risky, not just to me but to my family. We had a son in private school, a mortgage on our house, a rental property, and had already discussed potential plans for retirement. This move could change everything for us.

Mike and I had coffee a few more times while I was on sabbatical before he said he didn't think he could grow his business without me. He wanted me to be a part of his vision.

He promised me I would have complete autonomy and be his peer in operating the business. I had been very clear that I was not up for a subordinate role at this point in my career.

We talked openly about what we would need from one another to make this work, and there was complete mutual respect and transparency. After we reached an agreement on salary and bonus potential, discussions turned to my job title. Chief strategy officer was the most fitting, considering the role was a mix of planning for the future and improving daily operations. I was so excited, I could barely sit still.

Tate, however, was not enthusiastic about this idea.

I started working for Starbucks before he and I met, and it had been part of our lives for more than twenty-five years. I would be leaving behind a lot of equity, and he had reservations about me going to a very small business with limited growth and financial opportunity, even if it meant fulfilling my desire to be closer to my calling of helping others.

The shakiness of health care at the time added an additional layer of instability. With the future of the Affordable Care Act ambiguous, the industry was in turmoil, with disruption happening every day.

I was about to return to Starbucks from my sabbatical and was fully aware of what I was potentially giving up. But I was more excited about what was ahead and what I might gain from it. There are no guarantees in life, and I was ready to take a swing.

Tate and I spent hours talking about it over the course of an emotional couple of weeks, and his concerns weighed heavily on me—I didn't feel I could make this change without his complete support.

I was heartbroken. Generally supportive of my dreams, Tate was very reluctant about me making this move. We would be jumping into a big unknown, and it was starting to look like it wouldn't be feasible; it was just too dramatic a change for our family.

I regrettably texted Mike and told him that there had been a change in direction, and I didn't think we'd be able to move forward. I knew he couldn't pay me more, and I knew that my family relied on my income. I told him I'd get back to him after Tate and I had a chance to talk further, but my hopes were dimmed.

Rationally, I knew there would be plenty of additional opportunities for me beyond Tangelo, at Starbucks or somewhere else. That said, it was hard to extricate my emotions as I was already feeling committed to Tangelo and its future. I liked and trusted Mike and loved his team members. I had a personal connection to their mission because of my own injury, and I truly believed that they had an opportunity to make a difference in an antiquated industry.

After I texted Mike, I was still recovering from the disappointment during a weekend at our family cabin in the mountains, where Tate and I talked quite a bit about the opportunity at Tangelo and his concerns with me moving to a small company in an unknown industry. His trepidation was valid, and I felt I couldn't make the move without his unequivocal support.

It was quiet in the car on the way back to Seattle late Sunday afternoon. Nick had fallen asleep in the back seat while Tate was focused on driving the snow-covered roads. We sat in silence, except for the occasional snores emanating from the dogs sitting in the back seat next to Nick. Tate and I hadn't said much to each other since the previous evening, and tension hung heavy in the air.

I leaned against the car window with my eyes closed, conflicted and sad; the opportunity had faded, but I couldn't stop thinking about it. Every so often, I gazed up at the snow falling on the tall trees flanking the road and reflected on how pretty and quiet it was, the fresh snow muffling the road noise. There was a peaceful hush about everything.

It was Tate who broke the silence first.

"When I was on the chairlift this morning, I was thinking about our conversation last night." His voice was quiet and subdued. "Do what you want to do. I know you'll be successful at whatever you choose, and we will figure it out. If it doesn't work out, something else will come along. I believe in you."

I sat in disbelief for a moment. He had been so resistant the night before that I had mentally closed the door on Tangelo for good. I'm not sure what changed for Tate, but I was beyond grateful, and a shot of positive adrenaline went through me. His statement would change the course of our life.

Once we got back to Seattle, I texted Mike that I was in.

I kept my new gig to myself for a week and then finally gave my resignation to my boss, Andrew. His response was somewhat detached while he casually thanked me for my years of service with what felt like feigned genuineness.

The lackluster farewell on my last day when no one said a word and didn't seem to notice when I slipped out of the building confirmed that I had made the right decision.

* * *

Initially, it was strange being away from Starbucks. It had been my primary community and so enmeshed in my identity for a very long time. But I loved my new phase of life and exploration. Everything at Tangelo felt so fresh, and I was more excited about work than I had been in years. I was in a new industry, working with new people and energized by my new beginning.

I loved being surrounded by coworkers who had a deeply shared mission of helping others be healthy. I didn't see many Frappuccinos or baked goods in our office—my colleagues at Tangelo were more apt to be drinking kombucha, eating raw vegetables, or downing protein shakes. Even a team-building event at Tangelo meant a group workout of some sort.

Our purpose inspired me. People came to us when they were injured, often having tried everything they could to rehabilitate themselves. Oftentimes, we were a last resort before surgery or something else invasive.

Not only did we heal them, but we filled them with hope inside an environment of enthusiastic optimism. We helped them see that they could get better and stay better. When they finished their course of treatment, they were set free on a path toward unleashing their own potential, one that they may not have even envisioned yet.

I stayed connected to a few of my former Starbucks colleagues, and, when we got together, they surprised me by commenting on how happy I looked. I heard from others that I appeared "less stressed," and one friend even said that she thought I was the happiest person she knew.

I am generally an optimistic person, but "happy" wasn't a word I had heard much in recent years. It made me wonder if I was really that burned out before. Had I let work overtake my life in a way that wasn't healthy, or had I simply found more joy in my new job? I kind of wished I had before-and-after pictures of myself to see what they were talking about. But I didn't need to see a photo—I could feel it in my core.

Making the change had made me lighter and given me more energy. I was more present and available for my family. I wasn't so physically tired from ten-to-twelve-hour days even though I was getting up at the same time in the morning and going to bed at the same time in the evening. I was using my time differently now that I no longer had gruelingly long workdays.

There was a noticeable shift in me, and everyone else could see it.

My midlife clarity project ended up being not just about changing jobs but also about personal transformation.

Even though I was in a better place, it took some time to adjust to a small company. In an environment like that, everyone does pretty much everything, and there aren't many people to delegate to. I missed having a peer group to bounce ideas off of, so I made a conscious effort to maintain a cohort outside of the company that I could ask for help when needed.

The biggest adjustment was how I described to others where I worked and what I was doing. When I told someone I worked for Starbucks, no explanation was needed. But once I was at Tangelo, I had to explain what we did and who we were and then select a frame of reference that others might understand. I used analogies and descriptors such as physical therapy or sports medicine in the context of a high-energy community-oriented fitness studio.

It took some time for me to get comfortable with my new spiel about the business and why I decided to make the change.

It was almost as if I felt I had to justify to myself why I decided not to keep going after the next rung on the corporate career ladder. I was genuinely happy and didn't care about my financial future as much as I had previously, but I was living in the shadow of what I thought others expected of me.

I noticed myself a few times getting caught up in the whole thing I was trying to avoid—the idea that I should be following a certain path.

Eventually I learned to own my story and realized that the sum of my experiences and my character, not the company that I work for, define me.

It took my midlife clarity project and a subsequent leap into the unknown to teach me that.

CHAPTER 16

There's no better way to start the day than with a French press of freshly ground Starbucks Caffè Verona. Pure, roasty, and sweet, a blend of Indonesian and Latin American coffees with a touch of Italian Roast, Caffè Verona has been my favorite coffee since I first tasted it at my coffee-knowledge class at the Starbucks Roasting Plant in 1989. Of the thirty coffees we tasted in class that day, Caffè Verona rose to the top of my list as my favorite coffee at home and has stayed there ever since.

In anticipating my departure from Starbucks, I knew I had but one request from the company: I wanted to keep the benefit of a free weekly pound of coffee (termed the "markout") that I had been getting since I was a nineteen-year-old barista. It wasn't something I wanted because I wanted to save money on coffee at home; it was because the *ritual* of getting my weekly markout had been part of my life for almost thirty years.

Getting my markout each week was triggered by a note from Tate on the kitchen counter indicating we were nearly out of coffee. It simply said "coffee," scrawled in big letters on a piece of scratch paper to make sure I didn't miss it. He was the one who made the French press every morning and was highly attuned to our inventory levels. I'd take the note with me as I headed out the door to work and put it in a visible spot in my car as a reminder to stop at a store on my way home.

When Starbucks was much smaller and the corporate office was adjacent to the Roasting Plant, we were encouraged to go on the plant floor and scoop our markout beans ourselves. I would push open the door to the plant and deeply inhale the burned-toast-like smell of fresh roasted coffee as I made my way to the blue plastic markout bins.

I'd peruse the latest offerings and grab a bag to hand scoop what looked good to take home. After sealing the bag, I'd put a hash mark on a piece of paper hanging next to the bin to note that it was "marked out" of inventory.

By the time I left Starbucks, the only people who could retain the weekly markout benefit after they left the company were departing partners of retiring age. The policy stipulated that you must be age fifty-five or older and with the company for at least ten years. I had been with the company for almost three times the required tenure, but I was eight years shy of the age requirement. The idea of giving up my weekly markout for a new job surprisingly created the biggest sense of loss when I decided to leave Starbucks.

After I gave my notice, I spent my last couple of weeks making the rounds with some of the most senior executives in the company to let them know I was leaving and thank them for their mentorship and support over the years.

Each and every one of them asked if there was anything they could do for me on my way out. I told them without hesitation that my one request was to keep my markout, and I shared why—it was part of my life history. In the whole scheme of things, my ask was relatively small. I wasn't asking for an extension on my stock options or an exception made for my health benefits.

All the executives I met with said they'd do whatever they needed to support my request, but the final decision rested with David, the head of Partner Resources.

The day I finally met with David, I sat outside his office, waiting for him to finish another meeting. I crossed my fingers that he would instantly approve my seemingly inconsequential ask, but I knew from working in such a large company that it wouldn't be that simple.

While I was waiting, I took in the ever-changing over-the-top decor of his assistant's cubicle, which featured a constantly rotating color scheme. Everything from the lamps, file folders, throw pillows, and picture frames took on a new look about once per quarter. On this day, everything was a garish lime green, an obnoxious beacon among the rest of the neutral-toned cubicles around her.

Glancing through one of the windows into his office, I was still in awe of how big David's office was compared to other executive offices at Starbucks. Even though he was a direct report of Howard Schultz (the farther you went up the corporate ladder, the more square footage you had), he seemed to have lucked out because his office was one of the biggest in the building.

In addition to his desk, there were a large rustic wooden conference table and a weathered leather sofa flanked by red lambskin leather easy chairs. The walls were covered in burlap coffee bags, and the lighting fixtures looked like they came from Restoration Hardware. The whole look was shabby chic, meant to make you feel comfortable but not too cozy. It matched David's usual attire of expensive jeans, cashmere sweaters, and casual but well-made leather shoes.

He opened his door and welcomed me in. He knew I was making the rounds and was eager to hear why I was leaving and what I was going to be doing next.

After polite chitchat, David asked if there was anything he could do for me.

"Yes, there is. I have one request, and I understand that you are the one person who can grant it."

"Oh really?" he replied, a curious smile on his face. "What's that?"

"I'd like to keep my markout benefit. I know it's outside of company policy, but it's really important to me, so I have to ask. It's part of who I am and has been part of my life for such a long time."

"Well, what's the company policy on this?" I couldn't believe he didn't know, but figured it probably wasn't something he had come across during his two years with the company.

I patiently explained that I more than met the tenure requirements, but I wasn't old enough to officially retire from the company. He said he'd see what he could do and asked me to send him my request in writing along with the policy.

Walking out of his office, I highly doubted it was going to go anywhere. I could visualize the policy exception being caught up in the bureaucracy of corporate America, raising a bunch of questions no one could answer: Would this set a precedent? How would they track it? Were the systems in place to support it? How much would it cost? Which department would pay for it? My faith that I'd retain my markout faded, but at least I had asked.

As I neared my last day, David sent me an email indicating that he was still working on it. It wasn't a yes or a no, but I was still pretty sure it wasn't happening. I was one of over two hundred thousand partners and certainly not at the top of anyone's priority list, given all the other issues that come up in a company the size of Starbucks. I had never before asked to be treated as special or to have an exception made for me, but, in this case, I was hoping Starbucks would come through.

I was disappointed in David's noncommittal answer but not completely surprised.

Two weeks after I left, I had heard nothing and started buying full-priced coffee produced by other roasters. I felt like I was cheating on Starbucks, but I guess you could say I was protesting a bit—I had one small ask, and if they couldn't honor it after all my years of service, then screw them.

I sent David a follow-up note and let him know that I had been buying coffee and was wondering the status of my pending benefit. He told me that they were considering my request as a "potential pilot program" in which I'd be the inaugural participant, but they were still working out the details. After that email, I knew that the idea had gotten lost in the machinations of the SSC. It was time to move on.

The following week, I learned that David had been let go and was no longer with the company. In all my time at Starbucks, the head Partner Resources position was a revolving door, the longest-lasting executive in the position staying seven years, so I wasn't all that surprised.

With David out of the picture, I decided to take one last kick at the can and sent an email to the two most senior leaders I was closest to, Angela, a Partner Resources executive, and John, the head of Starbucks Asia. Maybe, just *maybe*, they could have a level of influence on my behalf.

In my email, I explained that David had been working on my request and I had recently heard he was no longer with the company. I reiterated why I wanted to keep my markout.

I pressed Send and held my breath. If it wasn't meant to be, it wasn't meant to be.

Less than twenty-four hours later, I got a reply from Angela that stopped me in my tracks: "Your partner number has been turned back on." The six digits assigned to me when I was first hired in 1989, the digits known as my partner number, would enable me to receive a free pound of coffee each week plus a 30 percent discount on food, beverages, and merchandise in any company-operated store for the rest of my life.

I cried with disbelief, happy tears spilling down my cheeks. Not only would I be getting my markout, but I'd be getting the standard partner discount as well.

My loyalty to Starbucks was reinstated and even deepened with this gesture.

The next day, I went into a store and was a little nervous as I stepped up to the register, fearing that my partner number wouldn't work. When the barista scanned my card and the transaction went through, a smile of relief and gratitude broke out on my face. The entire store team cheered when they heard my story.

What I didn't know at the time was that my idea sparked a flame inside the company about ways to honor tenured partners for their loyalty and commitment to the organization.

A cryptic text tipped me off about six months later: "I heard I have you to thank" read the brief message.

I didn't have the contact saved in my phone and didn't know who was sending me the obtuse message, so I played along and replied, "You are welcome, but thank me for what?"

He identified himself as Andrew, a vice president in the Coffee department. I smiled. Andrew and I were direct peers when I was on special assignment working on the Global Leadership Conference, and we spent many hours together sipping coffee and swapping leadership advice and coaching.

Andrew's next text was a screenshot of the announcement for a new company benefit. Starbucks had created a new program called the Silver Siren for partners who had been with the company for twenty-five years or more. Anyone who met that criteria would now receive their markout and partner discount for life, whether or not they were of retirement age.

I was moved. I had no idea this would happen and was so glad I never gave up. What had initially been a self-serving request would now benefit those who came after me.

The hurt and sadness I felt on my last day were still there, but gratitude and appreciation softened the edges.

To this day, every time I get my markout, I remind myself that the preservation of my personal ritual that starts with a note on my kitchen counter will forever be part of my legacy as a former partner.

And all I had to do was ask.

CHAPTER 17

On the one-year anniversary of my last day at Starbucks, I found myself walking into the Spanish Ballroom at the Fairmont Olympic Hotel along with many former colleagues. I was a little anxious because I hadn't been around so many current and former Starbucks partners since I resigned twelve months prior.

I left on good terms with the company but was still scarred from my last few weeks there. The fact that Andrew never acknowledged my last day, or even said thank you, lives with me to this day.

I was there to attend an event honoring Howard Behar, Starbucks's former president, who had since retired. Howard significantly shaped the culture of Starbucks during his tenure, putting people above all else. He was a disciple of servant leadership and emphatically believed that the sole purpose of a leader is to take care of the people around them. That night, Howard was deservedly receiving a Lifetime Achievement Award from the *Puget Sound Business Journal* for leadership excellence.

I loved Howard, and he had been mentoring me as I worked on this book, but I wasn't sure if I was ready to be thrust into a large group of Starbucks partners or alumni.

However, the idea of celebrating Howard's legacy and his impact on hundreds of thousands of Starbucks partners made it worth overcoming my own baggage to put on a smiling face and show support, if not for everyone else, then at least for him.

About a week prior to the event, a former coworker, Mary, called to see if I wanted to attend the banquet for Howard and sit at her table.

"Who else is attending?" I asked, and she chuckled. She knew a bit about the circumstances of my departure and named some former Starbucks partners and some newer ones I didn't know. In a nutshell, I would be safe, and there would be no one in attendance I wanted to avoid.

"Okay, I'll come, but only if I can sit next to you," I said. I needed her as my security blanket; I didn't want to be at a banquet table with people I didn't know or people I did know but who might stir up old feelings.

She told me that the event was semiformal, and we laughed again, this time because I'd have to trade my now-daily Tangelo wardrobe of yoga pants and sneakers for something more appropriate.

It had been a while since I dressed up, and I selected a sleeveless blouse, black slacks, and strappy heels complemented with a fresh pedicure. I looked healthy and happy and reminded myself that, while Starbucks was a large part of my identity, I had capably moved on and was thriving.

I was now comfortable with describing Tangelo and why I left Starbucks, and I felt confident and secure. Tonight, I could just be me—I didn't have to show up at this event worried about my career, trying to get face time with certain executives, or occupying myself with any political maneuvering.

Even so, I had nerves in my stomach when I dropped my car off with the valet and made my way up the escalator. I headed directly to the restroom to freshen up and collect myself. My palms were sweating, and I hadn't even made it to the reception area yet.

When I finally made my way into the ballroom, I felt out of place. At first, I didn't recognize a soul among the hundreds of people. Executives and leaders from other organizations were also being honored that evening, so the group of attendees was diverse.

Soon I spotted the familiar faces of former friends and partners from my early days at Starbucks. We exchanged warm greetings, caught up on our lives, and shared stories about Howard Behar. There was a natural connection among us, given all that we experienced together to grow the company. I relaxed even more because it started to feel like Old Home Week.

After getting a drink, I made a beeline for Jack Rodgers, a retired Starbucks executive I hadn't seen in years. I was bursting with gratitude and wanted to tell him the impact he had on me right after I left Starbucks.

I'd been gone from the company about a week and was driving Nick home from school. My phone rang, and the incoming call popped up on my display screen with a number I didn't recognize. I almost didn't answer, but something compelled me to pick it up.

"Hello, this is Christine," I answered with the guarded professionalism I used when I didn't know who was calling.

"Is this Chrissy Parr?" the somewhat shaky, deep male voice on the other end asked.

"Yes, but I haven't been called that in a while." I smiled with curiosity because I still didn't know who it was.

"This is a blast from the past, Jack Rodgers," the mystery voice answered. "Do you remember me?"

My jaw dropped, and my eyes widened. As mentioned earlier, Jack Rodgers was one of Starbucks's original investors, and we met when I started as a Human Resources coordinator working for Emily at our Seattle Roasting Plant office in 1991. It was my first corporate job, and he had an office down the hall from my cubicle.

His job was a mystery to me, but I knew that senior leaders turned to him for guidance, and he was a company culture keeper with a part-time schedule. Unbeknownst to me at the time, Jack often sat in the boardroom at Starbucks during earnings calls, up until Howard Schultz retired, and he still serves as a mentor and adviser to him.

"Of course I remember you!" I replied giddily.

A huge grin spread on my face, and I gestured incredulously to Nick, pointing at the phone and mouthing, "Oh my god."

Nick didn't know whom I was talking to, but a small smile crept onto his face in response—he could tell by the way I was acting that someone special was on the phone.

Jack and I talked for about twenty minutes and caught up on all that had happened over the years. He asked about my family and wanted to know when Chrissy Parr became Christine McHugh and what I had been doing at Starbucks before I left. I learned that his wife, Nancy, had suffered a stroke in recent years. While it was difficult for them both to move out of their home and into assisted living, they were together and adjusting.

At some point during the phone call, I found myself telling Jack about a memorable trip to Costco with him more than twenty-five years earlier.

We were working together to plan a party for the partners at the office and the Seattle Roasting Plant, and he and I were in charge of buying beverages and snacks for the event. Even though we were a small company, it still seemed odd that Jack would be assigned the task.

As we walked out of the store, he told me he had always wanted to try a Costco hot dog—he had heard they were good and wanted to see for himself.

After we loaded up on condiments, we made our way back to his pristine Cadillac because every table inside the store was full of people on their lunch break. I settled cautiously into the cushy, white leather seats, holding on to my hot dog tightly, nervous about leaving an evidence trail of ketchup and mustard where I sat.

Jack, on the other hand, ate his with gusto, claiming it was the best hot dog he had ever had—the Costco dog had lived up to its reputation.

I was in awe of the whole experience. Here I was, twenty-two years old, sitting next to an important and very down-to-earth executive, eating hot dogs as if we were just two normal people.

There were no hierarchical dynamics at play, and, in that moment, Jack taught me that being relatable as a leader goes a long way.

When I shared this memory with Jack over the phone, he started laughing.

"Well, Chrissy, I don't remember that, but I've had plenty of Costco hot dogs since then."

Jack said that he heard I'd left Starbucks and tracked me down through Howard Schultz's assistant, who had sent Jack my farewell email and a photo of me.

He told me that he called specifically to thank me for my dedication to Starbucks and for what I had contributed during my twenty-seven years of employment.

I was so appreciative and almost in tears because of his thoughtfulness and kindness. After we hung up, I couldn't stop smiling.

Jack's small but meaningful gesture made my day, my week, and my life. My last day with Starbucks had been one of the worst days of my Starbucks tenure, and when I walked out the doors of the Support Center, I was *done*.

But Jack's call made the world right again. His actions embodied the spirit of the Starbucks I once knew, and his genuineness demonstrated the humanity the company was built on.

On our way into the ballroom for the award ceremony, Jack asked me to sit next to him at dinner, and I would have wished for nothing else. The rest of our table was filled mostly with newer partners I didn't recognize, and there was only one empty seat next to Mary's left. I found myself grateful for the comfort of Mary's company, and I suspect Jack felt the same. Neither one of us knew many people at our table, and having a former coworker there was soothing.

I felt so at ease and empowered and in a completely different headspace than when I walked in the door. The nervous anticipation I felt at home when I dug out the cocktail attire from the back of my closet had dissipated.

Never before had I felt so much like myself in the presence of such esteemed company. Now that I was no longer a Starbucks partner, there wasn't anything for me to lose. My time away and the process of writing this book had boosted my confidence and self-assurance. I owned who I was, not someone I thought I should be.

I studied Jack as he talked to Mary. It had been years since I'd seen him. In one sense, he looked the exact same as when I first met him: a shock of white hair and heavy black glasses framing a face that lit up with enthusiasm when he heard something that pleased him.

He told me that he was eighty-six years old now and starting to feel it. I could tell he was slowing down a bit, but he was still the same curious and genuine Jack.

Between speeches, I leaned over to him and asked him how his wife was doing since we'd last talked. He said he was thrilled to be at the event for Howard but had never been away from her for such a long period of time. I was glad to be next to him to support him and help him enjoy this rare evening away. I grabbed his hand and let him know that I was so happy he could come and to let me know if I could do anything for him during the evening.

I took the opportunity to thank him once again for his phone call that week after I left the company and mentioned that I was hurt when my former manager didn't acknowledge my leaving. I skipped the specifics because I sensed Jack could tell that it wasn't handled well, and I didn't want to drag the evening down with unnecessary details.

He said he was glad that his call had such a positive impact on me, and I could see happy tears form in his eyes beyond the thick lenses of his glasses.

After capturing the moment with some selfies, we turned to watch and listen to the speeches by some of the other award winners being recognized that night while we ate our dinner.

We'd finished dessert, and it was getting close to the presentation of Howard Behar's award, the last of the evening.

I heard a buzz in the room and noticed that Howard Schultz had quietly slipped in and sat in the empty chair on the other side of Mary. The emcee announced his arrival, and I could see people turning to catch a glimpse of him, a local celebrity who had put Seattle on the map for coffee culture and the world headquarters of yet another globally recognized brand.

Howard hadn't been expected there that evening because he was in Italy, but apparently, he came back early to attend the event. He asked Mary if she would switch seats with him so that he could sit next to Jack and, by the look on Jack's face, I could tell he was ecstatic to see Howard.

Howard seemed just as excited to see Jack; their love was deep for one another. I could hear Howard share that he had come straight from the airport; he was tired and jetlagged. Jack nodded with approval and thanked Howard for making it a priority. This glimpse into the intimacy between the two of them gave me a peek into their decades-old mentee-mentor relationship.

When it was time for Howard Behar to receive his award, I watched Howard Schultz walk up to the podium.

Goose bumps rose on my arms as he regaled Howard Behar for all he did to establish the people-centered culture Starbucks became known for.

From cutting-edge benefits, to acts of grace for partners in need, to always ensuring that the partner voice was heard, Howard Behar never wavered from his commitment to setting the standard for how corporations should treat their people. As a businessperson, father, and husband, he consistently lived his values and stood by the principles of leadership he had steadfastly committed himself to. Directly and indirectly, Howard had significantly influenced the leader that I became—one dedicated to caring for people.

After Howard Behar's heartfelt acceptance speech on the importance of servant leadership, the crowd rose to give him a standing ovation.

On the escalator down to the hotel lobby, I felt at peace, and my heart was full. Here it was, exactly one year to the day that I glanced up at the clock tower to say goodbye to the Starbucks siren.

That last day had been full of anger and resentment, but, on this evening, I was surrounded by the culture, heritage, and spirit of Starbucks that had meant so much to me for so many years.

It felt like the circle had softly closed, like it was all meant to happen exactly that way. I could now let go and move forward, embracing life as a former partner.

I was a barista who made it all the way to the boardroom.

ACKNOWLEDGMENTS

Like most things in life, writing a book takes a village. It's not a solo effort by any means. There are those who have contributed to my story along my journey, those who have listened to me labor over the writing process, and those who have helped me get better each day to get this book to the finish line. And, thank you, reader, for letting me share part of my life with you. I am grateful for each person's contribution, small and large. You are my village.

There's no way I could have written this book or could have the stories within it without Tate. A steady and enthusiastic partner in my adventures, Tate has been my biggest cheerleader and supporter. I'd also like to thank our son, Nick, for teaching me how to be a mom, enduring my annoying mom habits, and for inspiring me to run my first 5k race. None of us knew at the time what running would become to me, but it changed my life.

Speaking of running, I'd also like to thank my good friend Subbu Sundaresan who prompted me to write this book in the first place. Many years ago, on one of our Saturday long runs, Subbu and I were swapping stories, and he suggested I write a book. At first, I scoffed as I didn't think I had a story that others would be interested in, but the idea settled in the back of my brain and wouldn't go away thanks to Subbu's relentless pestering. He's provided me with thoughtful feedback and insight on many drafts and has remained a loyal fan. I fully expect him to buy one hundred copies.

A special shout-out goes to Howard Behar, Starbucks's retired president and author of two books himself. Howard's encouragement and support, and his coaching and mentorship on the book-writing process kept me focused. His consummate modeling of servant-leadership principles has inspired me to deepen my own learning and practice in this area.

Tom Haro imprinted my leadership style like no one else, and I'm deeply grateful that he spotted my potential in my early twenties. His belief in me transformed my career in ways I never imagined possible, and he taught me to lead with empathy and the importance of building strong, trusting relationships with my team. I'm forever indebted to him and consider him a close friend and mentor.

To my editor, Andrea Nelson, I have the deepest gratitude. After our first conversation, she really got *me* and my story and over the course of our two years working together, successfully pulled out the writer who was buried deep inside me. Under her tutelage, my confidence flourished.

I'm grateful for the support of so many friends and family who cheered me on and checked in on my progress. You kept me going even when I didn't want to. Thank you.

ABOUT THE AUTHOR

Christine McHugh is an executive coach, consultant, and former Fortune 200 leader with hands-on experience, including twenty-seven years at Starbucks. She partners with leaders looking to scale their organizations, bringing a wealth of experience in strategic planning, operations, and culture development. She is president of the board for the Green Apron Alliance, a global nonprofit organization for Starbucks alumni. Christine began running in her early forties, when her then-elementary-age son invited her to participate in a 5K. She has completed four full marathons. Christine lives in Seattle with her husband, Tate, and son, Nick, and enjoys well-prepared cups of French-pressed Starbucks Caffè Verona.

CPSIA information can be obtained
at www.ICGtesting.com
Printed in the USA
FSHW010950140921
84759FS